CPAG'S

Housing Benefit and

Council Tax Benefit

Legislation

26th Edition

2013/2014

Supplement

Commentary by
Carolyn George MA
Richard Poynter BCL, MA(Oxon), District Tribunal Judge, Judge of the Upper Tribunal
Stewart Wright MA, Dip. Law, Barrister, Judge of the Upper Tribunal
Martin Williams Welfare rights worker, CPAG

Statutory instruments up to date to **31 May 2014**

Published by CPAG, 94 White Lion Street, London N1 9PF

CPAG promotes action for the prevention and relief of poverty among children and families with children. To achieve this, CPAG aims to raise awareness of the causes, extent, nature and impact of poverty, and strategies for its eradication and prevention; bring about positive policy changes for families with children in poverty; and enable those eligible for income maintenance to have access to their full entitlement. If you are not already supporting us, please consider making a donation, or ask for details of our membership schemes, training courses and publications.

Published by Child Poverty Action Group
94 White Lion Street, London N1 9PF
Tel: 020 7837 7979
staff@cpag.org.uk
www.cpag.org.uk

© Child Poverty Action Group 2014

This book is sold subject to the condition that it shall not, by way of trade or otherwise, be lent, resold, hired out or otherwise circulated without the publisher's prior consent in any form of binding or cover other than that in which it is published and without a similar condition including this condition being imposed on the subsequent purchaser.
A CIP record for this book is available from the British Library

Main work: ISBN 978 1 906076 80 1

Supplement: ISBN 978 1 906076 81 8

Child Poverty Action Group is a charity registered in England and Wales (registration number 294841) and in Scotland (registration number SC039339), and is a company limited by guarantee, registered in England (registration number 1993854). VAT number: 690 808117

Design by Devious Designs
Content management system by Konnect Soft www.konnectsoft.com
Typeset by David Lewis XML Associates Limited
Printed and bound by CPI Group (UK) Ltd, Croydon, CR0 4YY

Contents

Acknowledgements	iv
Table of Cases	v
Table of Upper Tribunal and Commissioners' decisions	vi
How to use this supplement	vii

PART I: NOTER UP

PART II: SECONDARY LEGISLATION

The Rent Officers (Housing Benefit and Universal Credit Functions) (Local Housing Allowance Amendments) Order 2013	21
The Age-Related Payments Regulations 2013	27
The Council Tax Reduction Schemes (Prescribed Requirements) (England) (Amendment) Regulations 2013	28
The Marriage (Same Sex Couples) Act 2013 (Consequential Provisions) Order 2014	31
The Housing Benefit (Transitional Provisions) (Amendment) Regulations 2014	33
The Housing Benefit (Miscellaneous Amendments) Regulations 2014	34
The Social Care (Self-directed Support) (Scotland) Act 2013 (Consequential Modifications and Savings) Order 2014	37
The Housing Benefit (Habitual Residence) Amendment Regulations 2014	39
The Marriage (Same Sex Couples) Act 2013 (Consequential and Contrary Provisions and Scotland) Order 2014	40
The Social Security (Miscellaneous Amendments) Regulations 2014	42
The Housing Benefit and Universal Credit (Supported Accommodation) (Amendment) Regulations 2014	45
The Social Security (Habitual Residence) (Amendment) Regulations 2014	47

Acknowledgements

This Supplement to the 26th edition provides commentary on all relevant new caselaw and updates to the legislation to 31 May 2014.

Thanks to Nicola Johnston for editing and managing the production of this book and to Mike Hatt at David Lewis XML.

Comments on this Supplement and the main work are always welcomed and can be sent to the authors via CPAG.

Carolyn George, Richard Poynter, Stewart Wright and Martin Williams

Table of cases

Camden LB v NW and SSWP (HB) [2011] UKUT 262 (AAC)... **7**
Hockenjos v Secretary of State for Social Security (No 2) [2004] EWCA Civ 1749, reported as R(JSA) 2/05... **8**
Humphreys v Revenue and Customs [2012] UKSC 18; [2012] AACR 46... **7**
Obrey and Others v SSWP [2013] EWCA Civ 1584... **6**
R (Mahmoudi) v London Borough of Lewisham and another [2014] EWCA Civ 284... **5**
R (MA and Others) v SSWP [2014] EWCA Civ 13... **6**
R (on the application of SG and others) v SSWP [2014] EWCA Civ 156... **9**
Saker v Secretary of State for Social Security [1988] 16 January *The Times*... **9**

Table of Upper Tribunal and Commmissioners' decisions

AA v Chesterfield BC [2011] UKUT 156 (AAC)... **6**
AD v Information Commissioner and Devon CC [2013] UKUT 550 (AAC)... **13**
AG v HMRC (TC) [2013] UKUT 530 (AAC)... **14**
BB v SSWP (ESA) [2014] UKUT 55 (AAC)... **14**
Bolton MBC v BF (HB) [2014] UKUT 48 (AAC)... **4**
Bury MBC v DC (HB) [2011] UKUT 43 (AAC)... **5**
CH 2201/2002... **5**
CH 3857/2004... **5**
CH 1363/2006... **5**
CH 2483/2012... **6**
CIS 3655/2007... **9**
CP v City of Brighton and Hove (HB) [2013] UKUT 543 (AAC)... **9**
DM v Lewisham LB and SSWP (HB) [2013] UKUT 26 (AAC)... **5**
DP v Mid Suffolk DC (HB) [2013] UKUT 93 (AAC)... **11**
DTM v Kettering Borough Council (CTB) [2013] UKUT 625 (AAC)... **12, 13**
GM v SSWP (JSA) [2014] UKUT 57 (AAC)... **11**
Guildford BC v MW (HB) [2014] UKUT 49 (AAC)... **8**
IB v Information Commissioner and Dorset Police [2013] UKUT 582 (AAC)... **15**
JP v SSWP (IS) [2014] UKUT 17 (AAC)... **3**
JS v Hull City Council [2012] UKUT 477 (AAC)... **9**
JS v SSWP and Cheshire West and Chester BC (HB) [2014] UKUT 36 (AAC)... **6**
JS v Kingston upon Hull City Council (HB) [2014] UKUT 43 (AAC)... **15**
KO v SSWP (ESA) [2013] UKUT 544 (AAC)... **15**
LA v Bury MBC (HB) [2013] UKUT 546 (AAC)... **7**
London Borough of Islington v JM (HB) [2014] UKUT 23 (AAC)... **11, 12**
MG v Carmarthenshire CC and SSWP (HB) [2013] UKUT 363 (AAC)... **4**
PP v Basildon DC (HB) [2013] UKUT 505 (AAC)... **3**
R(H) 4/07... **5, 6**
R(IS) 2/08... **11**
SL v SSWP and KL-D [2014] UKUT 128 (AAC)... **13**
Sunderland City Council v GH (HB) [2014] UKUT 3 (AAC)... **5**
TA v LB Islington (HB) [2014] UKUT 71 (AAC)... **9**
TD v SSWP and LB Richmond-upon-Thames (HB) [2013] UKUT 642 (AAC)... **8**
TM v HMRC (TC) [2013] UKUT 444 (AAC)... **15**

How to use this supplement

Use the Noter-up to find out about changes to the main volume. The page numbers on the left refer to pages in the main volume. The entry opposite either states what the change is or refers to another part of this supplement where the amending legislation is set out.

For abbreviations, see the table on pxlii of the main volume.

PART I:

NOTER-UP

General Note

The HB amounts for, for example, personal allowances, premiums, components, non-dependant deductions and deductions from rent are confirmed/uprated by the Social Security Benefits Uprating Order 2014 SI No.516 and the Welfare Benefits Uprating Order 2014 SI No.147 as from 1 April 2014 (7 April 2014 if rent is payable weekly or in multiples of a week).

The council tax reduction amounts in Scotland in the the Council Tax Reduction (Scotland) Regulations 2012 and the Council Tax Reduction (State Pension Credit) (Scotland) Regulations 2012 are uprated by The Council Tax Reduction (Scotland) Amendment Regulations 2014 SSI 2014 No.35 as from 1 April 2013.

The council tax reduction amounts in England in the Council Tax Reduction Schemes (Prescribed Requirements) (England) Regulations 2012 are uprated by the Council Tax Reduction Scheme (Prescribed Requirements) (England) (Amendment) Regulations 2013 SI No.3181 and Council Tax Reductions Schemes (Prescribed Requirements) (England) (Amendment) Regulations 2014 SI No.448 for schemes for financial years beginning on or after 1 April 2014.

The council tax reduction amounts in Wales in the Council Tax Reduction Schemes and Prescribed Requirements (Wales) Regulations 2013 and the Council Tax Reductions Schemes (Default Scheme)(Wales) Regualtions 2013 are uprated by the Council Tax Reduction Scheme (Prescribed Requirements and Default Schemes) (Wales) (Amendment) Regulations 2014 SI No.66 as from 15 January 2014.

pp12-18   SSCBA 1992 s137 – Interpretation of Part VII and supplementary provisions

In England and Wales, the definition of 'couple' substituted and para (1A) omitted by Art 2 and Sch 1 para 22 of the Marriage (Same Sex Couples) Act 2013 (Consequential and Contrary Provisions and Scotland) Order 2014 SI No.560 as from 13 March 2014.

[p14: In the Analysis, at the end of the paragraph starting 'Unmarried couple: para (b).' add:]

Note also that in *PP v Basildon DC (HB)* [2013] UKUT 505 (AAC), Judge Jacobs decided that although the 'signposts' remain relevant, they are not exhaustive and an analysis of the evidence needs to recognise the importance of the emotional aspect of the relationship between the parties.

[p15: In the Analysis, at the end of the paragraph starting 'Not civil partners: para (d).' add:]

In *JP v SSWP (IS)* [2014] UKUT 17 (AAC), a claimant who owned her home jointly with a person of the same sex was deemed to be a member of a couple for IS purposes with her joint owner. The claimant had described her joint owner as a friend and carer. However, the First-tier Tribunal decided she was a member of a couple as she and her joint owner were living together as if they were civil partners. In granting leave to appeal, Judge Levenson suggested that if two people have not entered into a civil partnership and maintain that they are not living together as civil partners, a high degree of proof is required to establish that they are living together. In allowing the claimant's appeal he said (at para 33):

> 'It seems to me that in cases involving a suggestion that a couple are living together as if they were husband and wife or as though they were civil partners the current state of the law is that a committed emotional loving relationship must be established and publicly acknowledged...An unacknowledged relationship cannot be the equivalent of marriage or a registered civil partnership which are, in their very nature, public acknowledgement of an emotional relationship. In the case of same sex relationships...some of the traditional signposts are of less assistance. It is for those alleging that two people are a couple within the meaning of section 137(1) to prove that there is a publicly acknowledged committed emotional loving relationship.'

pp43-46   SSAA 1992 s109B – Power to require information

The Social Security (Persons Required to Provide Information) Regulations 2013 SI No.1510 prescribe descriptions of people for the purpose of subsection (2)(ia).

Noter-up

pp173-74 TCEA 2007 s7 – Chambers: jurisdiction and Presidents

[p174: In the last paragraph of the General Note add:]

From 2 June 2014, the President of the Social Entitlement Chamber is Judge Aitken.

pp218-38 HB Regs reg 2 – Interpretation

Definition of 'couple' substituted by Sch 1 para 40 of the Marriage (Same Sex Couples) Act 2013 (Consequential Provisions) Order 2014 SI No.107 as from 13 March 2014.

Definition of 'young individual' amended by reg 3(2) of the Housing Benefit (Miscellaneous Amendments) Regulations 2014 SI No.213 as from 1 April 2014 (7 April if rent payable weekly or in multiples of a week).

Definition of 'service user group' omitted and para (5) – relating to 'service users' – inserted by reg 8(2) of the Social Security (Miscellaneous Amendments) Regulations 2014 SI No.591 as from 28 April 2014.

[p236: In the Analysis of the definition of 'person who requires overnight care', after the paragraph starting 'In addition, ...', add new paragraphs as follows:]

In *MG v Carmarthenshire CC and SSWP (HB)* [2013] UKUT 363 (AAC), the claimants had night carers who worked on a 'wakeful' system – ie, a carer was awake at night to see to their care needs as required. An additional room was provided for the use of the carers, but this was an office which did not contain a bed or facilities for sleeping. The local authority only allowed the single room rate of HB on the basis that the carers had not been provided with the use of a bedroom additional to those used by the people who occupied the dwelling as a home. The claimants' representative argued the word 'bedroom' should be read as extending to any room occupied by a carer providing night time care, whether or not the room contains a bed or is used for sleeping in. The appeal was dismissed on the basis that the room used by an overnight carer had to be in a fact bedroom.

Bolton MBC v BF (HB) [2014] UKUT 48 (AAC) concerned the meaning of 'bedroom' in paragraph (b). The claimant occupied a two-bedroom dwelling with his wife. The local authority accepted that the claimant required someone to provide him with overnight care, that he had arranged for and received such care and that his home had an extra bedroom. However, it decided that he was only entitled to one bedroom under the relevant size criteria (in his case those in reg 13D) because, for health reasons, he slept in the second bedroom, not his overnight carer, and his carer (his daughter) slept on a portable bed in the lounge. The First-tier Tribunal decided that the claimant did come within the definition of 'person who requires overnight care' and that his HB should be calculated based on the two-bedroom local housing allowance rate. The local authority appealed. Upper Tribunal Judge West dismissed the appeal. Considering the ordinary meaning of 'bedroom', he concluded that the claimant's carer had been provided with the use of a bedroom additional to those used by the people who occupied the dwelling as a home (ie, the claimant and his wife). The fact that the room his daughter used was also the lounge did not preclude it from being a bedroom. He distinguished the case from *MG v Carmarthenshire CC and SSWP (HB)*. He said:

> 'The legislation does not require that the "bedroom" must be a room primarily intended for sleeping in, such that a lounge or other living room is necessarily precluded from being a bedroom because it can be used for another purpose when it is not being used to be slept in. ... [T]he fact that the bed may have been folded up or put away in the course of the day when the room was being used as a lounge or living room does not mean that it was not a bedroom within the meaning of the regulations when [the carer] slept in it at night. It is sufficient if the room in question, of which the overnight carer has use, is furnished with a bed or is used for sleeping in. It would therefore make no difference if the claimant's daughter had, for example, slept on the sofa, or in a sleeping bag on cushions on the floor, as opposed to sleeping on a portable bed.'

pp247-59 HB Regs reg 7 – Circumstances in which a person is or is not to be treated as occupying a dwelling as his home

[p255: Under the heading 'Paragraphs (8) and (9): Delays in moving into new home', replace the first paragraph with:]

Like paragraph (6)(d), these paragraphs deal with the situation where a claimant has moved house, but this provision does not authorise the treatment of more than one dwelling as the claimant's home: only para (6) lists the situation in which this is possible. In *CH 2201/2002*, the judge decided that if an award of HB in respect of the former home had not been superseded, there was no power for the local authority to award HB for the new home under para (8) for an overlapping period. Thus, unless para (6) applied, para (8) could only apply to people who were not receiving HB in respect their former home. However, in *Sunderland City Council v GH (HB)* [2014] UKUT 3 (AAC), Judge Mark declined to follow *CH 2201/2002*. The claimant had claimed HB for a new home, but then delayed moving in while awaiting a payment from the social fund. She continued to receive HB for the refuge in which she resided. It was accepted that in respect of the new home, para (8)(c)(ii) applied to her, but she was not a person who could be entitled to HB for more than one home so the local authority did not award HB for the new home until she moved in. The judge decided that the claimant was entitled to HB for her new home for the four weeks prior to her move on the basis that the new home was the dwelling she occupied as her home for HB purposes, rather than the refuge. He said that if *CH 2201/2002* was correct in finding that a local authority has no power to make an HB award if it has failed to terminate an earlier one, it would follow that, even if a claimant moved home but the local authority in error failed to supersede the HB award in respect of the former home, so long as that error continued, there would be no power to make an award in respect of the new home. Note that as a consequence, HB was overpaid in respect of the claimant's former home. In such situations, as the judge pointed out, the local authority can suspend payment of HB pending a decision on which of the two dwellings the claimant occupies as her/his home, and for which of these HB should therefore be awarded.

[p255: Under the heading 'Paragraphs (8) and (9): Delays in moving home', for the paragraph numbered (4) and the following paragraph, substitute the following:]

(4) One or more of the conditions in para (8)(c)(i)-(iii) must be fulfilled.

Under para (8)(c)(i), the delay in moving must be necessary in order to adapt the dwelling to meet specified disablement needs. *CH 3857/2004* confirms the, perhaps obvious, point that the adaptations have to meet the needs of the claimant or family member which arise from or are particular to her/his disabilities (eg, handrails), rather than being works which would be necessary regardless of disability. This was emphasised in *R(H) 4/07*, where the commissioner followed an earlier decision of his (*CH 1363/2006*) in holding that the word 'adapt' entails a change to the fabric or structure of the dwelling and so did not encompass furnishing (eg, carpeting) or decorating the dwelling.

In *Bury MBC v DC (HB)* [2011] UKUT 43 (AAC) the claimant, due to his obsessive compulsive disorder, could not move into his new home until it had been redecorated and carpeted. Judge Jacobs decided that 'disablement' included mental as well as physical disablement. He considered whether 'necessary' meant 'essential' or 'reasonably required' and decided it meant the latter. However, following *R(H) 4/07*, he concluded that the works required in this case did not amount to adaptations of the dwelling. He considered whether the condition could be satisfied if the works that are needed have to be done in a way that takes account of the claimant's disability but concluded that this was not sufficient to bring a case within the provision. He said: 'It is the adapting of the dwelling that has to be necessary, not the manner in which it may have to be carried out.'

Judge Mesher, in *DM v Lewisham LB and SSWP (HB)* [2013] UKUT 26 (AAC), rejected arguments that *R(H) 4/07* was wrongly decided and said that, subject to human rights arguments, the meaning of regulation 7(8)(c)(i) was to be regarded as settled at the level of the Upper Tribunal. He then went on to consider whether the interpretation of 'adapt the dwelling' adopted in *R(H) 4/07*, and other decisions, discriminated against disabled people contrary to Article 14 of the European Convention on Human Rights (the ECHR) in conjunction with Article 8 (right to respect for private and family life) and/or Article 1 of Protocol 1 (protection of property). Judge Mesher decided that there was a not a difference of treatment on the ground of a personal characteristic under Article 14 of the ECHR, but in any event, even on the assumption that the claimant's case under that article did not fail, the difference of treatment of the claimant was objectively and reasonably justified, so that there was no contravention of Article 14. The claimant appealed to the Court of Appeal in *R (Mahmoudi) v London Borough of Lewisham and another* [2014] EWCA Civ 284, 6

February 2014. The Court considered the meaning of 'adapt the dwelling' and concluded that reg 7(8)(c) cannot have been intended to exclude a disabled person who is unable to move into her/his home while it is being decorated to meet her/his disablement needs but to include one who is, for example, unable to move in while the bathroom and kitchen are being refitted to meet her/his disablement needs. It agreed with the approach the First-tier Tribunal suggested it would have followed had it not been constrained by *R(H) 4/07*, that adapt 'can mean to make fit, to change or modify to suit a purpose. What in any individual case will amount to adapting a dwelling to meet the disablement needs of a person will depend very much on the nature of those needs. Adapting a dwelling need not ... involve works of any particular type and specifically need not involve any physical interference with the structure of the dwelling or any physical addition to it. Provided the result of the process which the dwelling has undergone is that it has been changed to make it more suitable for the needs of the disabled person, it can fairly be said to have been adapted.'

[p258: In the Analysis to 'Paragraphs (13) and (16) to (17): Temporary absence', for the final sentence in the paragraph numbered (ii), substitute the following:]

The claimants' appeal against the decision of the Upper Tribunal was unsuccessful: *Obrey and Others v SSWP* [2013] EWCA Civ 1584, 5 December 2013. It is understood that an appeal to the Supreme Court is being considered.

pp282-83   HB Regs reg 10 – Persons from abroad

Para (3B) amended by reg 2 of the Housing Benefit (Habitual Residence) Amendment Regulations 2014 SI No.539 as from 1 April 2014.

Subparas (a)-(f) of para (3B) substituted by reg 5 of the Social Security (Habitual Residence) (Amendment) Regulations 2014 SI No.902 as from 31 May 2014.

p341   HB Regs reg A13 – When a maximum rent (social sector) is to be determined
Para (1) amended by reg 3 of the Housing Benefit (Transitional Provisions) (Amendment) Regulations 2014 SI No.212 as from 3 March 2014.

pp342-46   HB Regs reg B13 – Determination of maximum rent (social sector)

[p346: In the fifth paragraph of the Analysis to paras (6) and (7), for the final sentence starting 'It is understood ...' substitute the following:]

The claimants' appeal to the Court of Appeal was unsuccessful: *R(MA and Others) v SSWP* [2014] EWCA Civ 13, 21 February 2014.

pp354-61   HB Regs reg 13D – Determination of a maximum rent (LHA)

[p358: After the first paragraph in the Analysis to 'Para (2)(b): One bedroom self-contained accommodation', add a new paragraph:]

JS v SSWP and Cheshire West and Chester BC (HB) [2014] UKUT 36 (AAC) concerned the meaning of the phrase 'has the exclusive use of' in reg 13D(2) HB(SPC) Regs (which is identical to reg 13D HB Regs). The judge considered whether it meant rooms a person practically has control over and sole use of (a 'practical control test') or, as found by the First-tier Tribunal, a legal right to exclude others from the rooms. He said that the correct starting point was ascertaining the meaning of the phrase in the context of the statutory scheme within which it appears, and that the context must include reading reg 13D(2) together with the relevant terms of the Rent Officers (Housing Benefit Functions) Order 1997. He rejected the claimant's argument that as a matter of law or a matter of approach the starting point is that the phrase 'exclusive use' has to be given a non-technical and ordinary meaning. Agreeing with Judge Wikeley's opinion in *AA v Chesterfield BC*, which was followed by the judge in *CH 2483/2012*, he concluded that 'exclusive use' means the legal right to exclude others from the rooms and not, as the claimant contended, as a matter of fact or practice has the sole use of the rooms.

[p360: For the final two sentences in the paragraph starting 'In the wake of the judgment ...' substitute:]

In *LA v Bury MBC (HB)* [2013] UKUT 546 (AAC), Judge Mark considered the appropriate remedy in an appeal against a decision denying an extra bedroom for a disabled child who could not share a bedroom that pre-dated the amendment to the HB Regs. In *obiter* remarks, the Court in *R(MA and others)* had said (at para 93) that compliance with *Burnip, Trengove* and *Gorry* is not a local authority's legal responsibility. Judge Mark said he was unable to understand how this could be compatible with the duties of a local authority under s6 HRA 1998. The Court of Appeal in *Burnip* did not construe the HB Regs as entitling those in the claimant's position to an additional payment for an extra bedroom. The finding in *R(MA and others)* was that the local authority retained its discretion in relation to discretionary housing payments, suggesting that it could properly refuse such a grant. He said:

> '13. The Court of Appeal in its judgments declined to do more that grant declaratory relief, and left it to the Secretary of State as to how to deal with the rectification of the discrimination in the three cases before it. In doing so, it stated that it was following the approach in *Francis v SSWP*, [2006] 1 WLR 3202, where the Court of Appeal had found that the inability of a claimant to obtain a maternity grant under the terms of the regulations then in force amounted to discrimination contrary to article 14 of the Human Rights Convention. The Court of Appeal in that case found that it was not possible to construe the relevant regulation to include the claimant and simply declared that the claimant was entitled to a maternity grant, leaving it to the Secretary of State to decide how best to reformulate the regulations.
>
> 14. The confusion as to the appropriate remedy appears to be resolved once one considers the actual relief granted in Burnip and in Gorry and the third case before the Court of Appeal, Trengrove v Walsall. Paragraph 3 of the order reads as follows:
>
>> 'The decision in each case is remitted to the First Respondent in each case [i.e. the relevant council] to be remade in accordance with the Court of Appeal's judgment. Each Appellant is entitled to have their case reassessed by the First Respondent in each case, and to receive from the First Respondent payment of such further sum (in addition to any discretionary housing payment or other relevant payment already made) as is necessary to comply with this judgment and Article 14 for the period to which the appeal relates.'
>
> 15. It is plain from this order that notwithstanding the wording of the judgments of the Court of Appeal, the actual order did impose an obligation on the relevant councils to make the necessary payments notwithstanding that regulation 13D precluded a full award of housing benefit under the Housing Benefit Regulations.
>
> 16. It is also plain as a result that the Divisional Court in MA was wrong to state that the council only had a discretion to make such payments, being unaware that, despite the wording of the judgments of the court, the Court of Appeal had actually made an order which did impose an immediate obligation on the councils in question to comply with Article 14. This approach is also supported by Francis.'

Judge Mark, therefore, approached the question of remedy in the same way as the Court of Appeal and decided that the claimant was entitled to payment of a sufficient amount in addition to anything payable under the HB Regs that would result in her and her family not being discriminated against contrary to Article 14. For it to comply with Article 14, the local authority had to determine whether the claimant was entitled to an additional amount, if so how much and to pay it; it had no discretion in this.

pp371-72   **HB Regs reg 20 – Circumstances in which a person is to be treated as being or not being a member of the household**

[p372: For the final paragraph of the Analysis substitute:]

In *Camden LB v NW and SSWP (HB)* [2011] UKUT 262 (AAC), the claimant's attempt to challenge the use of the receipt of child benefit as a deciding factor in cases where a child spends exactly equal time in different households failed. The appeal was decided before the Supreme Court made its decision in *Humphreys v Revenue and Customs* [2012] UKSC 18; [2012] AACR 46. The Supreme Court rejected Human Rights Act arguments in the context of child tax credit, albeit in an appeal concerning a different rule than for HB, and not about exactly equal shared care.

Noter-up

TD v SSWP and LB Richmond-upon-Thames (HB) [2013] UKUT 642 (AAC) was an appeal by a father who had exactly equal care of his child but did not receive child benefit for him. He argued that the rule in reg 20(2)(a) HB Regs indirectly discriminated against men as fewer men than women in his situation received child benefit. The Upper Tribunal judge, having considered statistical evidence, agreed, but decided that the discrimination was justified; it could not be said that per *Humphreys* the discrimination was manifestly without reasonable foundation. The claimant's argument that the discrimination was not justified on the facts of his case because he was not seeking HB to be paid twice or for it to be apportioned (his child's mother was not an HB claimant) was rejected because what has to be justified is the indirectly discriminatory effects of the rule and not its effect in any particular case, though the latter may inform the former.

Whether a challenge would fail where the claimant is a 'substantial minority carer' is yet to be decided – ie, where the child or young person does not spend equal time living with the claimant but, for example, stays with her/him for at least 104 nights a year: see, for example, *Hockenjos v Secretary of State for Social Security (No 2)* [2004] EWCA Civ 1749, reported as R(JSA) 2/05. However, the finding of justification in respect of reg 20(2)(a) generally in *TD* may make such arguments difficult.

pp385-89   HB Regs reg 28 – Treatment of child care charges
Paras (11) and (13) amended by reg 3(3) of the Housing Benefit (Miscellaneous Amendments) Regulations 2014 SI No.213 as from 1 April 2014 (7 April if rent payable weekly or in multiples of a week).

p397   HB Regs reg 34 – Disregard of changes in tax, contributions, etc
Para (c) and amended by reg 3(4) of the Housing Benefit (Miscellaneous Amendments) Regulations 2014 SI No.213 as from 1 April 2014 (7 April if rent payable weekly or in multiples of a week).

p398   HB Regs reg 35 – Earnings of employed earners
Para (2)(d) amended by reg 8(3) of the Social Security (Miscellaneous Amendments) Regulations 2014 SI No.591 as from 28 April 2014.

pp404-6   HB Regs reg 38 – Calculation of net profit of self-employed earners
Paras (1), (3) and (9) amended by reg 3(4) of the Housing Benefit (Miscellaneous Amendments) Regulations 2014 SI No.213 as from 1 April 2014 (7 April if rent payable weekly or in multiples of a week).

p408   HB Regs reg 39 – Deduction of tax and contributions of self-employed earners
Para (2) amended by reg 3(4) of the Housing Benefit (Miscellaneous Amendments) Regulations 2014 SI No.213 as from 1 April 2014 (7 April if rent payable weekly or in multiples of a week).

pp412-15   HB Regs reg 42 – Notional income
Para (12A) amended by reg 8(4) of the Social Security (Miscellaneous Amendments) Regulations 2014 SI No.591 as from 28 April 2014.

p420   HB Regs reg 44 – Calculation of capital
[p420: In the General Note, at the end of the second paragraph, add:]

The proper approach is to disregard (or consider disregarding) capital under Sch 6 without determining its value, rather than determining the value and then only considering whether the capital can be disregarded if it is above a relevant limit: *Guildford BC v MW (HB)* [2014] UKUT 49 (AAC).

p423   HB Regs reg 48 – Calculation of capital outside the United Kingdom
[p423: In the General Note, at the end of the second paragraph, add:]

An argument that the 'willing buyer' test in para (b) does not apply in cases of valuing property outside the United Kingdom was rejected in *Guildford BC v MW (HB)* [2014] UKUT 49 (AAC). The

Noter-up

local authority's arguement was that it does not apply because the words 'willing buyer' appear in regulation 46(b) of the HB Regs but not reg 46(a). However, the words have to be implied into the 'current market value' test. The judge said that the words 'willing buyer' are used explicitly in para (b) 'to make good the fictional ability to sell in the UK and to avoid the argument that there would be no willing buyer in the UK if there was such a prohibition.'

pp474-75   HB Regs Part 8A – Benefit cap

[p475: In the second paragraph of the General Note headed 'Challenging the benefit cap', substitute 'R (on the application of SG and others) v SSWP [2014] EWCA Civ 156, 21 February 2014' for the case reference. Then at the end of the paragraph add:]

Permission to appeal to the Supreme Court has been granted. The appeal was due to be heard on 29 and 30 April 2014.

p476   HB Regs reg 75C – Manner of calculating the amount of welfare benefits

Para (2)(a) amended by reg 3(2) of the Housing Benefit and Universal Credit (Supported Accommodation) (Amendment) Regulations 2014 SI No.771 as from 10 April 2014.

p476   HB Regs new reg 75H – Specified accommodation

New reg 75H inserted by reg 3(3) of the Housing Benefit and Universal Credit (Supported Accommodation) (Amendment) Regulations 2014 SI No.771 as from 10 April 2014.

p506   HB Regs reg 87 – Amendment and withdrawal of claim

Para (1) amended by reg 3(5) of the Housing Benefit (Miscellaneous Amendments) Regulations 2014 SI No.213 as from 1 April 2014 (7 April if rent payable weekly or in multiples of a week).

pp529-30   HB Regs reg 99 – Meaning of overpayment

[p529: Under the Analysis at the very bottom of p529, add a new paragraph:]

CP v City of Brighton and Hove (HB) [2013] UKUT 543 (AAC) makes the valuable, but much missed, point that there cannot be two or more separate overpayments covering the same period. If a local authority has made a decision that a claimant has been overpaid HB for a period due to, for example, failure to disclose an increase in her/his earnings, and the authority then identifies that the claimant's partner's earnings had also increased during the same period, the correct legal approach is not for it to make a separate overpayment decision arising from the partner's earnings but for it to revise the first overpayment decision so as to take account of this second basis for the overpayment over the period.

pp530-37   HB Reg 100 – Recoverable overpayments

[p535: After 'could not..... reasonably have been expected to realise', delete the first two sentences and the words 'This has' in the third sentence and replace with:]

The test here is subjective – ie, whether the particular person with her/his experience, abilities and education could reasonably have been expected to realise: *JS v Hull City Council* [2012] UKUT 477 (AAC) at para 16 and *TA v LB Islington (HB)* [2014] UKUT 71 (AAC) at para 14. This had

pp537-42 HB Reg 101 – Person from whom recovery may be sought

[p542: Delete the whole of the sentence following 'a material fact' and replace with:]

The better view may now arguably be that a 'material fact' is one that itself would justify a different outcome decision (per *CIS 3655/2007*) rather than the lesser test of a fact that might well have affected the decision (per *Saker v Secretary of State for Social Security* [1988] 16 January *The Times*, CA (reported as *R(I) 2/88)*).

pp575-91   HB Regs Sch 3 – Applicable amounts

Paras 13, 14, 15 and 16 amended by reg 3(6) of the Housing Benefit (Miscellaneous Amendments) Regulations 2014 SI No.213 as from 1 April 2014 (7 April if rent payable weekly or in multiples of a week).

Noter-up

pp607-24 HB Regs Sch 5 – Sums to be disregarded in the calculation of income other than earnings
Para 57 amended by Art 2 and Sch para 10 of the Social Care (Self-directed Support) (Scotland) Act 2013 (Consequential Modifications and Savings) Order 2014 SI No.513 as from 1 April 2014.

Para 2A amended by reg 8(5) of the Social Security (Miscellaneous Amendments) Regulations 2014 SI No.591 as from 28 April 2014.

pp624-40 HB Regs Sch 6 – Capital to be disregarded
Para 58 amended by Art 2 and Sch para 10 of the Social Care (Self-directed Support) (Scotland) Act 2013 (Consequential Modifications and Savings) Order 2014 SI No.513 as from 1 April 2014.

pp657-68 HB (SPC) Regs reg 2 – Interpretation
Definition of 'couple' substituted by Sch 1 para 41 of the Marriage (Same Sex Couples) Act 2013 (Consequential Provisions) Order 2014 SI No.107 as from 13 March 2014.

Definition of 'service user group' omitted and para (6) – relating to 'service users' – inserted by reg 9(2) of the Social Security (Miscellaneous Amendments) Regulations 2014 SI No.591 as from 28 April 2014.

pp677-79 HB(SPC) Regs reg 10 – Persons from abroad
Subparas (a)–(f) of para (4A) substituted by reg 6 of the Social Security (Habitual Residence) (Amendment) Regulations 2014 SI No.902 as from 31 May 2014.

pp707-11 HB(SPC) Regs reg 31 – Treatment of child care charges
Paras (11) and (13) amended by reg 4(2) of the Housing Benefit (Miscellaneous Amendments) Regulations 2014 SI No.213 as from 1 April 2014 (7 April if rent payable weekly or in multiples of a week).

p713 HB(SPC) Regs reg 34 – Disregard of changes in tax, contributions etc
Para (d) amended by reg 4(3) of the Housing Benefit (Miscellaneous Amendments) Regulations 2014 SI No.213 as from 1 April 2014 (7 April if rent payable weekly or in multiples of a week).

p714 HB(SPC) Regs reg 35 – Earnings of employed earners
Para (2)(f) amended by reg 9(3) of the Social Security (Miscellaneous Amendments) Regulations 2014 SI No.591 as from 28 April 2014.

pp717-18 HB(SPC) Regs reg 39 – Calculation of net profit of self-employed earners
Paras (1), (2) and (8) amended by reg 4(3) of the Housing Benefit (Miscellaneous Amendments) Regulations 2014 SI No.213 as from 1 April 2014 (7 April if rent payable weekly or in multiples of a week).

pp718-19 HB(SPC) Regs reg 40 – Deduction of tax and contributions of self-employed earners
Para (2) amended by reg 4(3) of the Housing Benefit (Miscellaneous Amendments) Regulations 2014 SI No.213 as from 1 April 2014 (7 April if rent payable weekly or in multiples of a week).

pp719-21 HB(SPC) Regs reg 41 – Notional income
Para (8C) amended by reg 9(4) of the Social Security (Miscellaneous Amendments) Regulations 2014 SI No.591 as from 28 April 2014.

pp721-22 HB(SPC) Regs reg 42 – Income paid to third parties
Para (3) amended by reg 9(5) of the Social Security (Miscellaneous Amendments) Regulations 2014 SI No.591 as from 28 April 2014.

p749 HB(SPC) Regs reg 68 – Amendments and withdrawal of claim
Para (1) amended by reg 4(4) of the Housing Benefit (Miscellaneous Amendments) Regulations 2014 SI No.213 as from 1 April 2014 (7 April if rent payable weekly or in multiples of a week).

Noter-up

pp778-83   HB(SPC) Regs Sch 3 – Applicable amounts
Paras 6, 7 and 8 amended by reg 4(4) of the Housing Benefit (Miscellaneous Amendments) Regulations 2014 SI No.213 as from 1 April 2014 (7 April if rent payable weekly or in multiples of a week).

pp791-98   HB(SPC) Regs Sch 6 – Capital to be disregarded
Para 26D amended by Art 2 and Sch para 11 of the Social Care (Self-directed Support) (Scotland) Act 2013 (Consequential Modifications and Savings) Order 2014 SI No.513 as from 1 April 2014.

pp827-29   RO(HBF) Order Sch 3B – Broad rental market area determinations and local housing allowance determinations
Para 2 substituted and para 6 inserted by Art 2 of the The Rent Officers (Housing Benefit and Universal Credit Functions) (Local Housing Allowance Amendments) Order 2013 SI No.2978 as from 13 January 2014.

pp846-48   RO(HBF) (Scotland) Order Sch 3B – Broad rental market area determinations and local housing allowance determinations
Para 2 substituted and para 6 inserted by Art 3 of the The Rent Officers (Housing Benefit and Universal Credit Functions) (Local Housing Allowance Amendments) Order 2013 SI No.2978 as from 13 January 2014.

pp859-61   D&A Regs reg 1 – Citation, commencement and interpretation
Definition of 'couple' substituted by Sch 1 para 30 of the Marriage (Same Sex Couples) Act 2013 (Consequential Provisions) Order 2014 SI No.107 as from 13 March 2014.

pp872-75   D&A Regs reg 4 – Revision of decisions
Para (7H) inserted by reg 3(2) of the Benefit Cap (Housing Benefit) Regulations 2012 SI No.2994 as from 15 April 2013.

pp872-75   D&A Regs reg 7 – Decisions superseding earlier decisions
Para (2)(i) amended and para (2)(s) inserted by reg 2(2) of the Housing Benefit (Miscellaneous Amendments) Regulations 2014 SI No.213 as from 3 March 2014.

pp878-80   D&A Regs reg 8 – Date from which a decision superseding an earlier decision takes effect
Para (14G) inserted by reg 2(3) of the Housing Benefit (Miscellaneous Amendments) Regulations 2014 SI No.213 as from 3 March 2014.

pp892-93   D&A Regs reg 17 – Appeal against a decision which has been revised

[p892: At the end of the paragraph beginning 'Therefore, in the example…', add:]

However, R(IS) 2/08 is not authority for the proposition that an appeal only lapses if the revising decision has given the appellant everything s/he could have obtained from the appeal: see *London Borough of Islington v JM (HB)* [2014] UKUT 23 (AAC) at para 42.

[p893: At the end of the Analysis, add the following sentence and new paragraph:]

However, the decision in *DP v Mid Suffolk DC (HB)* must now be read in the light of the decision in *GM v SSWP (JSA)* [2014] UKUT 57 (AAC) in which the Upper Tribunal appears to have accepted (eg, at para 10) that 'merely substituting one ground for disallowance for another should not cause an appeal to lapse'.

It is sometimes disputed whether the First-tier Tribunal and Upper Tribunal have jurisdiction to second-guess a decision by a local authority that an appeal has lapsed. The answer is that they do (and, indeed, the decision in *R(IS) 2/08* could not have been given if it were otherwise). As Judge Rowland put it in *GM v SSWP (JSA)* (at para 7):

'A ruling that an appeal has lapsed is in principle appealable (see *LS v LB Lambeth (HB)* [2010] UKUT 461 (AAC); [2011] AACR 27). I agree with the Secretary of State

Noter-up

that the First-tier Tribunal has no power to decide whether or not an appeal *should* lapse, because lapsing occurs automatically.... However, if there is a dispute as to whether an appeal has, by operation of law, lapsed, the First-tier Tribunal must rule on the issue and such a ruling is appealable.' (added emphasis)

Similarly, in *London Borough of Islington v JM (HB)*, it was stated (at para 38) that it is 'ultimately for the tribunal to decide whether – and to what extent – revision has occurred'. It might also have been said that it is for the First-tier Tribunal to decide whether the effect of a revising decision is 'more advantageous'.

p912-13   TP(FT)(SEC) Rules rule 8 – Striking out a party's case

[p912: At the end of the General Note, add:]

See further *DTM v Kettering Borough Council (CTB)* [2013] UKUT 625 (AAC).

[p912: In the Analysis under the heading 'Failure to comply with Directions: paras (1), (3)(a), (5) and (6)', after the second paragraph, add the following new paragraphs:]

In a social security appeal (including HB), the circumstances in which it will be appropriate to strike out an appeal under paras (1) or (3)(a) will be exceptional. In *DTM v Kettering Borough Council (CTB)*, Judge Poynter stated:

'57. The First-tier Tribunal's jurisdiction in relation to social security appeals is inquisitorial. When it is seised of an appeal, its primary duty is to decide that appeal on its merits. That is because giving a decision on the merits is usually the fairest and most just way of disposing of the proceedings. It is implicit in the requirement to seek to give effect to the overriding objective when exercising the power to strike out that that power should only be used in cases where striking out is a fairer, or more just, way of dealing with the appeal than giving a substantive decision.

58. The fact that the Tribunal's jurisdiction is inquisitorial means that the issues in a social security appeal are likely to be less clearly defined than they would be in adversarial proceedings. There are no pleadings and the Tribunal exercises an "enabling role". What that means is that claimants are entitled to rely upon the special expertise of the Tribunal to ensure that the law is correctly applied to the facts of their case even if they themselves do not raise all the issues which arise from the evidence (see the decision of the Court of Appeal of Northern Ireland in *Mongan v Department of Social Development* [2005] NICA 16 (reported as *R 4/01(IS)*) and endorsed by the Court of Appeal of England and Wales in *Hooper v Secretary of State for Work and Pensions* [2007] EWCA Civ 495 at paragraphs 25-28).

59. Given the complexity of the social security system, a just outcome would be impossible in many appeals if the Tribunal did not perform that role. Its existence is often cited as a reason why it is not necessary to extend legal aid to social security appeals (e.g., *Tribunals for Users: One System, One Service, the report of the review of tribunals by Sir Andrew Leggatt*, The Stationery Office, London, 2001).

60. The fact that claimants may rely upon the Tribunal's enabling role means that they are permitted to use the appellate process to ask the Tribunal to check whether a decision about their benefits is correct. Claimants will often, and understandably, be unaware of the detailed rules about entitlement to benefits and the respondent's decision-making procedures. They will often be unable to identify with any precision why they believe a decision is wrong. Rule 23(6)(e) of the Procedure Rules requires that an appeal should state the grounds on which the appellant relies, so claimants must give the best explanation they can, but, once they have done so, the rules do not require them to participate any further in the process unless the Tribunal so directs.

61. So if a claimant sets out his or her case in the notice of appeal and then waits for the Tribunal to give its decision, that is a legitimate use of the Tribunal's procedures – and, in particular, its enabling role – not a basis for striking out the appeal. A claimant who does so is not misusing those procedures in the same way as claimants in adversarial proceedings misuse the procedures of a court if they commence proceedings and then do not pursue them.

62. A further aspect of the Tribunal's inquisitorial jurisdiction in social security appeals is that the role of the respondent is not adverse to the claimant (see Diplock J. (as he then was) in *R. v Medical Appeal Tribunal (North Midland Region), ex parte Hubble* [1958] 2 QB 228 at 240 as approved by the House of Lords in *Kerr v Department of Social Development*, [2004] UKHL 23 (also reported as R 1/04 (SF)) at para.61). That is so whether the respondent is the Secretary of State, HM Revenue & Customs or a local authority.

63. Entitlement to social security benefits is conferred by Parliament as a matter of right on claimants who satisfy the conditions of entitlement. The authorities that administer those benefits must do their best to ensure that such claimants receive their proper entitlement. If they do not do so, the purpose of the legislation conferring the right to benefit is frustrated as much as it is if benefits are awarded to those who are not entitled to them. The role of a respondent to a social security appeal is therefore to help the Tribunal arrive at the correct decision. There is no legitimate interest in the maintenance of the decision under appeal if that decision is incorrect and usually no unfairness, or injustice, to the respondent if the First-tier Tribunal checks that the decision is correct rather than striking out the appeal without consideration of the issues.'

For examples of the practical problems that can result from use of the power of automatic strike out under para (1), see *DTM v Kettering Borough Council (CTB)* at paras 40-43 and 84 and *SL v SSWP and KL-D* [2014] UKUT 128 (AAC) at paras 12–15.

[p913: After the first paragraph under the heading 'Failure to co-operate, paras (3)(b) and (4)', add:]

For guidance on the exercise of the power conferred by para (3)(b), see *AD v Information Commissioner and Devon CC* [2013] UKUT 550 (AAC).

[p913: Delete the second paragraph (ie, beginning 'Under para (8)...') under the heading 'Barring respondents from further participation in the proceedings: paras (7) and (8)'.]

[p913: Delete final sentence under the heading 'Barring respondents from further participation in the proceedings: paras (7) and (8)' and add the following new paragraphs:]

In *SL v SSWP and KL-D*, Judge Jacobs gave detailed guidance about the effects of barring a respondent as follows.

'17. Rule 8 bars a party from taking further part in the proceedings. It does not operate retrospectively to render that which has already been done nugatory or invalid: rule 7(1). Evidence submitted and submissions made remain before the tribunal and have to be taken into account. When it provides that 'the Tribunal need not consider any response or other submission made by that respondent' it means any future response or submission.

18. Rule 8(8) provides that the tribunal 'may summarily determine any or all issues against that respondent.' This is not a penal provision. The tribunal cannot simply accept the appellant's case if the respondent is barred. It must still act in accordance with the overriding objective when considering whether to exercise this power. And it is, on basic principle as part of its duty to act fairly, required to act rationally on material of probative value in making its decision: *Mahon v New Zealand Ltd* [1984] AC 808 at 820-821 (Lord Diplock). This requires it to give proper consideration to submissions made and to take account of evidence submitted. The key word in rule 8(8) is summarily. It allows the tribunal to deal with the respondent's case rather more briefly than would otherwise be required.

19. The effect of rule 8 is to bar a respondent from participating in the proceedings. It does not remove that person as a party.

20. That means that a respondent barred from participating retains the right to appeal to the Upper Tribunal: section 11(2).

21. An application to the First-tier Tribunal for permission to appeal to the Upper Tribunal is a separate proceeding from the appeal itself: *Harkness v Bell's Asbestos and Engineering Ltd* [1967] 2 QB 729 at 735 (Lord Denning MR) and 736 (Diplock

Noter-up

LJ). To put it another way, barring only applies to the proceedings on the appeal. A party who is barred from participating may, therefore, nonetheless apply to the First-tier Tribunal for permission to appeal.

22. Even if that is wrong, barring under rule 8 applies only to the proceedings before the First-tier Tribunal: rule 1(2). It has no effect on the Upper Tribunal, which has power to waive any irregularity in its own rules as a result of a party's inability to apply for permission from the First-tier Tribunal: rule 7(2)(a).

23. When the Upper Tribunal sets aside a decision of the First-tier Tribunal and remits the case for reconsideration, the proceedings before the First-tier Tribunal are fresh proceedings. Any barring or strike out no longer operates. This follows from the rules of procedure, the nature of a rehearing and practical considerations.

24. As to the rules of procedure, they envisage that there comes a point at which proceedings on appeal are concluded. They do so by attaching consequences to the (final) disposal of the proceedings or of all the issues in the proceedings. See the definition of 'party' in rule 1(2), rule 17(1)(a) (withdrawal), rule 27(3) (striking out without a hearing), rule 33 (notice of decision), rule 34 (reasons for decision) and rule 37 (setting aside).

25. As to the nature of a rehearing, there is no provision for proceedings to revive following a successful appeal, whether in statute, in the rules of procedure, or on the general principles on the operation of appeals. If a case is remitted, the First-tier Tribunal considers the case afresh. The earlier proceedings are now past...'

pp914-15   TP(FT)(SEC) Rules rule 11 – Representatives

[p915: Before the first full paragraph on the page, insert the following new paragraphs:]

The decision of Judge Williams in *BB v SSWP (ESA)* [2014] UKUT 55 (AAC) highlights, perhaps unintentionally, an ambiguity in the wording of r11(6). The rule appears to operate prospectively – ie, any person who is given notice that a representative has been appointed must *in future* send any document that s/he would otherwise be required to send to the represented party to the representative instead. The additional provision that the person 'need not provide the document to the represented party' is *otiose* if the rule covers documents that have already been provided to that party in the past.

However, Judge Williams appears (the decision is brief and it is not entirely clear) to have interpreted the rule as meaning that documents that have been sent in the past to the party must be sent again to the representative. The judge stated that 'all relevant documents **must** be given to the representative once due notice is received' (original emphasis).

If that is what was intended, then it is doubted whether the decision is correct. The rule does not state that 'all relevant documents' must be provided to the representative. It says that documents which are 'required to be provided to the represented party' must be so provided. Where a document has been provided to a party in the past, any requirement to provide it ceases to exist. So, any document that has already been provided to the party before the appointment of the representative is no longer a document which is required to be provided to the represented party and, therefore, need not be provided to the representative.

Nevertheless, the decision in *BB v SSWP (ESA)* exists and may be of assistance to representatives who need to obtain duplicate copies of documents from the First-tier Tribunal.

pp922-24   TP(FT)(SEC) Rules rule 24 – Responses and replies

[p923: At the end of the first sentence under the heading 'Head (b):' add:]

'Document' is defined by r1(3) and means 'anything in which information is recorded in any form', including, for example, recordings of telephone calls which recorded information: see *AG v HMRC (TC)* [2013] UKUT 530 (AAC).

[Then continue with the existing second sentence ('The important words...') but as a new paragraph.]

Noter-up

[p924: Immediately before the heading 'Further submissions: paras (6) and (7)' add a new paragraph:]

Provision of response to other parties: para (5). In the absence of a direction to the contrary in an individual case, the local authority must always send a copy of the response to the other parties as well as to the First-tier Tribunal: see *TM v HMRC (TC)* [2013] UKUT 444 (AAC) at paras 5-7. If an authority wishes to absolve itself of its duty to provide its written appeal response to an appellant (or her/his representative or any other party to the appeal), it must first makes its case to the First-tier Tribunal and obtain a direction to that effect. It would be extremely rare for such a direction to be given.

p924-26   TP(FT)(SEC) Rules rule 27 – Decision with or without a hearing

[p925: At the end of the first full paragraph on the page, add:]

The duty to hold a hearing unless the appeal can be decided fairly and justly without one continues throughout the case: see *KO v SSWP (ESA)* [2013] UKUT 544 (AAC). In effect, the First-tier Tribunal cannot decide finally whether a hearing is needed until it knows what that decision would be and its reasons for reaching it.

[p925: At the beginning of the following paragraph, delete the words 'It is also necessary' and substitute:]

Consent is not the same thing as the absence of objection and there must be evidence that it has been positively given: see *IB v Information Commissioner and Dorset Police* [2013] UKUT 582 (AAC). Before reaching a decision without a hearing in a case where there has been no positive consent to that course, it is necessary

pp934-36   TP(FT)(SEC) Rules rule 40 – Review of a decision

[p934: Replace the third full paragraph of the General Note with:]

The view, expressed in previous editions, that the requirement that there should be an application for permission to appeal is *ultra vires* is incorrect: see *JS v Kingston upon Hull City Council (HB)* [2014] UKUT 43 (AAC). Rule 40(2)(a) is authorised by s22 and Sch 5 para 6 TCEA. The First-tier Tribunal has no power to review its decisions on its own initiative.

pp997-1003   The Council Tax Reduction Schemes (Prescribed Requirements) (England) Regulations 2012 reg 2 – Interpretation

Definition of 'enactment' amended by reg 2(2) of the Council Tax Reduction Scheme (Prescribed Requirements) (England) (Amendment) Regulations 2013 SI No.3181 for schemes for financial years beginning on or after 1 April 2014.

pp1003-04   The Council Tax Reduction Schemes (Prescribed Requirements) (England) Regulations 2012 reg 2 – Meaning of "pensioner" and "person who is not a pensioner"

Para (3)(a)(ii) amended by reg 2(3) of the Council Tax Reduction Scheme (Prescribed Requirements) (England) (Amendment) Regulations 2013 SI No.3181 for schemes for financial years beginning on or after 1 April 2014.

p1004   The Council Tax Reduction Schemes (Prescribed Requirements) (England) Regulations 2012 reg 4 – Meaning of "couple"

Reg 4 substituted by Sch 1 para 54 of the Marriage (Same Sex Couples) Act 2013 (Consequential Provisions) Order 2014 SI No.107 as from 13 March 2014.

pp1046-50   The Council Tax Reduction Schemes (Prescribed Requirements) (England) Regulations 2012 Sch 6 – Capital disregards

Para 29 amended and para 29ZA inserted by Art 2 and Sch para 22 of the Social Care (Self-directed Support) (Scotland) Act 2013 (Consequential Modifications and Savings) Order 2014 SI No.513 as from 1 April 2014.

Noter-up

pp1003-6 **The Council Tax Reduction Schemes (Prescribed Requirements) (England) Regulations 2012 reg 8 – Households**
Paras (2) and (5) amended by reg 2(4) of the Council Tax Reduction Scheme (Prescribed Requirements) (England) (Amendment) Regulations 2013 SI No.3181 for schemes for financial years beginning on or after 1 April 2014.

pp1007-8 **The Council Tax Reduction Schemes (Prescribed Requirements) (England) Regulations 2012 reg 12 – Persons treated as not in Great Britain**
Paras (4) and (5) amended by reg 2(5) of the Council Tax Reduction Scheme (Prescribed Requirements) (England) (Amendment) Regulations 2013 SI No.3181 for schemes for financial years beginning on or after 1 April 2014.

pp1008-9 **The Council Tax Reduction Schemes (Prescribed Requirements) (England) Regulations 2012 reg 13 – Persons subject to immigration control**
Para (1) amended and para (1A) inserted by reg 2(6) of the Council Tax Reduction Scheme (Prescribed Requirements) (England) (Amendment) Regulations 2013 SI No.3181 for schemes for financial years beginning on or after 1 April 2014.

pp1009-36 **The Council Tax Reduction Schemes (Prescribed Requirements) (England) Regulations 2012 Sch 1 – Pensioners: matters that must be included in an authority's scheme**
Para 2 heading and paras 6 and 25 amended by reg 2(7) of the Council Tax Reduction Scheme (Prescribed Requirements) (England) (Amendment) Regulations 2013 SI No.3181 for schemes for financial years beginning on or after 1 April 2014.

pp1041-43 **The Council Tax Reduction Schemes (Prescribed Requirements) (England) Regulations 2012 Sch 4 – Sums disregarded from applicant's earnings**
Para 3 amended by reg 2(10) of the Council Tax Reduction Scheme (Prescribed Requirements) (England) (Amendment) Regulations 2013 SI No.3181 for schemes for financial years beginning on or after 1 April 2014.

pp1047-50 **The Council Tax Reduction Schemes (Prescribed Requirements) (England) Regulations 2012 Sch 6 – Capital disregards**
Paras 21 and 22 amended and para 29A inserted by reg 2(12) of the Council Tax Reduction Scheme (Prescribed Requirements) (England) (Amendment) Regulations 2013 SI No.3181 for schemes for financial years beginning on or after 1 April 2014.

p1171 **The Council Tax Reduction Schemes and Prescribed Requirements (Wales) Regulations 2013 SI No.3029**
The regulations came into force on 28 November 2013, and apply in relation to council tax reduction schemes made by authorities for financial years beginning on or after 1 April 2014.

Regs 2, 8 and 28 and Sch 1 paras 10,11,14,19 and 24, Sch 5 paras 21 and 22, Sch 6 para 25, Sch 7 paras 1, 3 and 10, Sch 10 para 12 and Sch 11 paras 9 and 10 amended and Sch 5 para 33 and Sch 10 paras (2A) and 63 inserted by regs 2 to 12 of the Council Tax Reduction Schemes (Prescribed Requirements and Default Scheme) (Wales) (Amendment) Regulations 2014 SI No.66 as from 15 January 2014.

Sch 5 para 28 and Sch 9 paras 59 and 60 amended and Sch 5 para 28A inserted by Art 2 and Sch para 25 of the Social Care (Self-directed Support) (Scotland) Act 2013 (Consequential Modifications and Savings) Order 2014 SI No.513 as from 1 April 2014.

pp1171-292 **The Council Tax Reduction Schemes and Prescribed Requirements (Wales) Regulations 2012**
The regulations are revoked by reg 36 of the The Council Tax Reduction Schemes and Prescribed Requirements (Wales) Regulations 2013 SI No.3029 as from 1 April 2014.

Noter-up

p1293 **The Council Tax Reduction Schemes (Default Scheme) (Wales) Regulations 2013 SI No 3035**

The regulations came into force on 28 November 2013, and apply in relation to council tax reduction schemes made by authorities for financial years beginning on or after 1 April 2014.

Sch paras 8, 19, 55, 59, 64, 65, 70, 78, 79, 97 and 103, Sch 6 para 9, Sch 7 paras 32 and 40 and Sch 8 paras 21 and 22 amended and Sch 8 para 33 and Sch 9 paras (2A) and 63 inserted by regs 13 to 32 of the Council Tax Reduction Schemes (Prescribed Requirements and Default Scheme) (Wales) (Amendment) Regulations 2014 SI No.66 as from 15 January 2014.

Sch 7 para 59, Sch 8 para 28 and Sch 9 para 60 amended and Sch 8 para 28A inserted by Art 2 and Sch para 26 of the Social Care (Self-directed Support) (Scotland) Act 2013 (Consequential Modifications and Savings) Order 2014 SI No.513 as from 1 April 2014.

pp1293-402 **The Council Tax Reduction Schemes (Default Scheme) (Wales) Regulations 2012**

The regulations are revoked by reg 1(4) of the The Council Tax Reduction Schemes (Default Scheme) (Wales) Regulations 2013 SI No.3035 as from 1 April 2014.

p1646 **The Social Security (Penalty Notice) Regulations 1997**

Reg 2 amended by reg 5 of the Social Security (Miscellaneous Amendments) Regulations 2014 SI No.591 as from 28 April 2014.

pp1673-702 **HB&CTB(CP) Regs 2006 Sch 3 – Transitional and savings provisions**

Para 4 amended by reg 2 of the The Housing Benefit (Transitional Provisions) (Amendment) Regulations 2014 SI No.212 as from 3 March 2014.

PART II:
SECONDARY LEGISLATION

The Rent Officers (Housing Benefit and Universal Credit Functions) (Local Housing Allowance Amendments) Order 2013

(SI 2013 No.2978)

Made   25th November 2013
Coming into force   13th January 2014

The Secretary of State for Work and Pensions makes the following Order in exercise of the powers conferred by section 122(1) and (6) of the Housing Act 1996.

Citation and commencement

1. This Order may be cited as the Rent Officers (Housing Benefit and Universal Credit Functions) (Local Housing Allowance Amendments) Order 2013 and comes into force on 13th January 2014.

Amendment to the Rent Officers (Housing Benefit Functions) Order 1997

2.–(1) Schedule 3B (Broad rental market area determinations and local housing allowance determinations) to the Rent Officers (Housing Benefit Functions) Order 1997 is amended as follows.

(2) For paragraph 2 (Local housing allowance for category of dwelling in paragraph 1) substitute–

"**Local housing allowance for category of dwelling in paragraph 1**

2.–(1) Subject to paragraph 3 (anomalous local housing allowances), the rent officer must determine a local housing allowance for each category of dwelling in paragraph 1 as follows.

(2) For the broad rental market areas listed in column 1 of the table in paragraph 6 the local housing allowance is–
- (a) for a category of dwelling listed in column 2 in relation to that broad rental market area, either–
    - (i) the rate last determined increased by 4 per cent; or
    - (ii) the maximum local housing allowance for that category of dwelling listed in column (2) of the table in sub-paragraph (9) where that is lower than or equal to the rate last determined increased by 4 per cent;
- (b) for any category of dwelling not listed in column 2 of the table in paragraph 6 in relation to that broad rental market area, either–
    - (i) the rent at the 30th percentile determined in accordance with sub-paragraphs (4) to (8); or
    - (ii) the rate last determined for that category of dwelling increased by 1 per cent. where that is lower than or equal to the rent at the 30th percentile determined in accordance with sub-paragraphs (4) to (8).

(3) For all other broad rental market areas the local housing allowance for a category of dwelling is, either–
- (a) the rent at the 30th percentile determined in accordance with sub-paragraphs (4) to (8); or
- (b) the rate last determined for that category of dwelling increased by 1 per cent. where that is lower than or equal to the rent at the 30th percentile determined in accordance with sub-paragraphs (4) to (8).

(4) The rent officer must compile a list of rents in ascending order of the rents which, in the rent officer's opinion, are payable–
- (a) for a dwelling let under an assured tenancy for each category of dwelling specified in paragraph 1; and
- (b) in the 12 month period ending on the 30th day of the September preceding the date of the determination.

(5) In compiling the list of rents, the rent officer must–
- (a) include within it the rent of an assured tenancy in relation to each category of dwelling if–
    - (i) the dwelling let under the assured tenancy is in the broad rental market area for which the local housing allowance for that category of dwelling is being determined;
    - (ii) the dwelling is in a reasonable state of repair; and
    - (iii) the assured tenancy permits the tenant to use exclusively or share the use of, as the case may be, the same number and type of rooms as the category of dwelling in relation to which the list is being compiled;
- (b) include within it any rents which are of the same amount;
- (c) where rent is payable other than weekly, use the figure which would be payable if the rent were to be payable weekly by–
    - (i) multiplying the rent by an appropriate figure to obtain the rent for a year;

(ii) dividing the total in (i) by 365; and
(iii) multiplying the total in (ii) by 7;
(d) assume that no one who would have been entitled to housing benefit had sought or is seeking the tenancy; and
(e) exclude the amount of any rent which, in the rent officer's opinion, is fairly attributable to the provision of services performed for, or facilities (including the use of furniture) provided for, or rights made available to, the tenant which are ineligible to be met by housing benefit.

(6) Sub-paragraph (7) applies where the rent officer is not satisfied that the list of rents in respect of any category of dwelling would contain sufficient rents, payable in the 12 month period ending on the 30th day of the September preceding the date of the determination for dwellings in the broad rental market area, to enable a local housing allowance to be determined which is representative of the rents that a landlord might reasonably be expected to obtain in that area.

(7) In a case where this sub-paragraph applies the rent officer may add to the list rents for dwellings in the same category in other areas in which a comparable market exists.

(8) The rent officer must use the list of rents to determine the rent at the 30th percentile in the list ("R") by–
(a) where the number of rents on the list is a multiple of 10, applying the formula–

$$R = \frac{\text{the amount of the rent at P} + \text{the amount of the rent at P1}}{2}$$

Where–
(i) P is the position on the list found by multiplying the number of rents on the list by 3 and dividing by 10; and
(ii) P1 is the following position on the list;
(b) where the number of rents on the list is not a multiple of 10, applying the formula–

$$R = \text{the amount of the rent at P2}$$

Where–
P2 is the position on the list found by multiplying the number of rents on the list by 3 and dividing by 10 and rounding the result upwards to the nearest whole number.

(3) The maximum local housing allowance for each category of dwelling specified in the paragraph of this Schedule listed in column (1) is the amount specified for that category of dwelling in column (2).

(1) Paragraph of this Schedule defining the category of dwelling	(2) Maximum local housing allowance for that category of dwelling
paragraph 1(1)(a) (one bedroom, shared accommodation)	£258.06
paragraph 1(1)(b) (one bedroom, exclusive use)	£258.06
paragraph 1(1)(c) (two bedrooms)	£299.34
paragraph 1(1)(d) (three bedrooms)	£350.95
paragraph 1(1)(e) (four bedrooms)	£412.89

(10) Where the local housing allowance would otherwise not be a whole number of pence, it must be rounded to the nearest whole penny by disregarding any amount less than half a penny and treating any amount of half a penny or more as a whole penny.".

(3) After paragraph 5 insert–

"**6.** The table referred to in paragraph 2(2) of this Schedule is below.

(1) Broad rental market area	(2) Paragraph of this Schedule defining the category of dwelling
Ashford	paragraph 1(1)(a) (one bedroom, shared accommodation)
Aylesbury	paragraph 1(1)(a) (one bedroom, shared accommodation)
	paragraph 1(1)(d) (three bedrooms)
Barnsley	paragraph 1(1)(b) (one bedroom, exclusive use)
Bath	paragraph 1(1)(b) (one bedroom, exclusive use)
	paragraph 1(1)(c) (two bedrooms)
	paragraph 1(1)(d) (three bedrooms)
Bedford	paragraph 1(1)(b) (one bedroom, exclusive use)
	paragraph 1(1)(e) (four bedrooms)
Blackwater Valley	paragraph 1(1)(a) (one bedroom, shared accommodation)
Blaenau Gwent	paragraph 1(1)(a) (one bedroom, shared accommodation)
Bolton and Bury	paragraph 1(1)(a) (one bedroom, shared accommodation)
Brecon and Radnor	paragraph 1(1)(d) (three bedrooms)
Bridgend	paragraph 1(1)(a) (one bedroom, shared accommodation)
Brighton and Hove	paragraph 1(1)(d) (three bedrooms)

(SI 2013 No.2978, art 2)

Bristol	paragraph 1(1)(e) (four bedrooms)
Caerphilly	paragraph 1(1)(e) (four bedrooms)
Cambridge	paragraph 1(1)(a) (one bedroom, shared accommodation)
	paragraph 1(1)(b) (one bedroom, exclusive use)
	paragraph 1(1)(d) (three bedrooms)
	paragraph 1(1)(e) (four bedrooms)
Canterbury	paragraph 1(1)(e) (four bedrooms)
Central Lancs	paragraph 1(1)(a) (one bedroom, shared accommodation)
Central London	paragraph 1(1)(a) (one bedroom, shared accommodation)
Ceredigion	paragraph 1(1)(a) (one bedroom, shared accommodation)
	paragraph 1(1)(b) (one bedroom, exclusive use)
Cheltenham	paragraph 1(1)(a) (one bedroom, shared accommodation)
Cherwell Valley	paragraph 1(1)(b) (one bedroom, exclusive use)
	paragraph 1(1)(c) (two bedrooms)
	paragraph 1(1)(e) (four bedrooms)
Chesterfield	paragraph 1(1)(a) (one bedroom, shared accommodation)
Chichester	paragraph 1(1)(a) (one bedroom, shared accommodation)
Coventry	paragraph 1(1)(c) (two bedrooms)
Crawley & Reigate	paragraph 1(1)(e) (four bedrooms)
Derby	paragraph 1(1)(a) (one bedroom, shared accommodation)
Durham	paragraph 1(1)(a) (one bedroom, shared accommodation)
East Cheshire	paragraph 1(1)(e) (four bedrooms)
East Thames Valley	paragraph 1(1)(c) (two bedrooms)
	paragraph 1(1)(d) (three bedrooms)
Exeter	paragraph 1(1)(a) (one bedroom, shared accommodation)
Gloucester	paragraph 1(1)(a) (one bedroom, shared accommodation)
High Weald	paragraph 1(1)(d) (three bedrooms)
Hull & East Riding	paragraph 1(1)(a) (one bedroom, shared accommodation)
Inner East London	paragraph 1(1)(a) (one bedroom, shared accommodation)
	paragraph 1(1)(b) (one bedroom, exclusive use)
Inner North London	paragraph 1(1)(a) (one bedroom, shared accommodation)
Inner South East London	paragraph 1(1)(a) (one bedroom, shared accommodation)
	paragraph 1(1)(b) (one bedroom, exclusive use)
	paragraph 1(1)(c) (two bedrooms)
	paragraph 1(1)(d) (three bedrooms)
	paragraph 1(1)(e) (four bedrooms)
Inner South West London	paragraph 1(1)(a) (one bedroom, shared accommodation)
	paragraph 1(1)(b) (one bedroom, exclusive use)
	paragraph 1(1)(c) (two bedrooms)
Inner West London	paragraph 1(1)(a) (one bedroom, shared accommodation)
	paragraph 1(1)(b) (one bedroom, exclusive use)
	paragraph 1(1)(c) (two bedrooms)
Lancaster	paragraph 1(1)(a) (one bedroom, shared accommodation)
Leeds	paragraph 1(1)(a) (one bedroom, shared accommodation)
Luton	paragraph 1(1)(a) (one bedroom, shared accommodation)
	paragraph 1(1)(c) (two bedrooms)
	paragraph 1(1)(d) (three bedrooms)
Maidstone	paragraph 1(1)(a) (one bedroom, shared accommodation)
Mendip	paragraph 1(1)(e) (four bedrooms)
Merthyr Cynon	paragraph 1(1)(a) (one bedroom, shared accommodation)
Mid & East Devon	paragraph 1(1)(a) (one bedroom, shared accommodation)
	paragraph 1(1)(b) (one bedroom, exclusive use)
Mid & West Dorset	paragraph 1(1)(a) (one bedroom, shared accommodation)
Mid Staffs	paragraph 1(1)(a) (one bedroom, shared accommodation)
Neath Port Talbot	paragraph 1(1)(a) (one bedroom, shared accommodation)
Newbury	paragraph 1(1)(a) (one bedroom, shared accommodation)
North Cornwall & Devon Borders	paragraph 1(1)(a) (one bedroom, shared accommodation)
North Nottingham	paragraph 1(1)(b) (one bedroom, exclusive use)
North West Kent	paragraph 1(1)(a) (one bedroom, shared accommodation)
North West London	paragraph 1(1)(a) (one bedroom, shared accommodation)
	paragraph 1(1)(b) (one bedroom, exclusive use)
	paragraph 1(1)(c) (two bedrooms)
	paragraph 1(1)(d) (three bedrooms)
	paragraph 1(1)(e) (four bedrooms)
North West Wales	paragraph 1(1)(e) (four bedrooms)
Northampton	paragraph 1(1)(a) (one bedroom, shared accommodation)

Outer East London	paragraph 1(1)(a) (one bedroom, shared accommodation)
	paragraph 1(1)(b) (one bedroom, exclusive use)
	paragraph 1(1)(c) (two bedrooms)
	paragraph 1(1)(d) (three bedrooms)
	paragraph 1(1)(e) (four bedrooms)
Outer North London	paragraph 1(1)(a) (one bedroom, shared accommodation)
	paragraph 1(1)(b) (one bedroom, exclusive use)
	paragraph 1(1)(c) (two bedrooms)
	paragraph 1(1)(e) (four bedrooms)
Outer South London	paragraph 1(1)(d) (three bedrooms)
	paragraph 1(1)(e) (four bedrooms)
Outer South West London	paragraph 1(1)(a) (one bedroom, shared accommodation)
	paragraph 1(1)(c) (two bedrooms)
	paragraph 1(1)(d) (three bedrooms)
	paragraph 1(1)(e) (four bedrooms)
Oxford	paragraph 1(1)(d) (three bedrooms)
Rotherham	paragraph 1(1)(c) (two bedrooms)
Scarborough	paragraph 1(1)(a) (one bedroom, shared accommodation)
Sheffield	paragraph 1(1)(a) (one bedroom, shared accommodation)
South Cheshire	paragraph 1(1)(b) (one bedroom, exclusive use)
	paragraph 1(1)(c) (two bedrooms)
South East Herts	paragraph 1(1)(b) (one bedroom, exclusive use)
South Gwynedd	paragraph 1(1)(a) (one bedroom, shared accommodation)
Southampton	paragraph 1(1)(a) (one bedroom, shared accommodation)
Southern Greater Manchester	paragraph 1(1)(d) (three bedrooms)
Staffordshire North	paragraph 1(1)(a) (one bedroom, shared accommodation)
Taff Rhondda	paragraph 1(1)(a) (one bedroom, shared accommodation)
Thanet	paragraph 1(1)(a) (one bedroom, shared accommodation)
Walton	paragraph 1(1)(a) (one bedroom, shared accommodation)
	paragraph 1(1)(e) (four bedrooms)
Warwickshire South	paragraph 1(1)(d) (three bedrooms)
West Wiltshire	paragraph 1(1)(e) (four bedrooms)
Wolds and Coast	paragraph 1(1)(a) (one bedroom, shared accommodation)
Worcester North	paragraph 1(1)(a) (one bedroom, shared accommodation)
Worcester South	paragraph 1(1)(a) (one bedroom, shared accommodation)
Yeovil	paragraph 1(1)(a) (one bedroom, shared accommodation)".

Amendment to the Rent Officers (Housing Benefit Functions) (Scotland) Order 1997

3.–(1) Schedule 3B (Broad rental market area determinations and local housing allowance determinations) to the Rent Officers (Housing Benefit Functions) (Scotland) Order 1997 is amended as follows.

(2) For paragraph 2 (Local housing allowance for category of dwelling in paragraph 1) substitute–

"**Local housing allowance for category of dwelling in paragraph 1**

2.–(1) Subject to paragraph 3 (anomalous local housing allowances)(d), the rent officer must determine a local housing allowance for each category of dwelling in paragraph 1 as follows.

(2) For the broad rental market areas listed in column 1 of the table in paragraph 6 the local housing allowance is–
  (a) for a category of dwelling listed in column 2 in relation to that broad rental market area, either–
    (i) the rate last determined increased by 4 per cent; or
    (ii) the maximum local housing allowance for that category of dwelling listed in column (2) of the table in sub-paragraph (9) where that is lower than or equal to the rate last determined increased by 4 per cent.
  (b) for any category of dwelling not listed in column 2 of the table in paragraph 6 in relation to that broad rental market area, either–
    (i) the rent at the 30th percentile determined in accordance with sub-paragraphs (4) to (8); or
    (ii) the rate last determined for that category of dwelling increased by 1 per cent. where that is lower than or equal to the rent at the 30th percentile determined in accordance with sub-paragraphs (4) to (8).

(3) For all other broad rental market areas the local housing allowance for a category of dwelling is either—
- (a) the rent at the 30th percentile determined in accordance with sub-paragraphs (4) to (8); or
- (b) the rate last determined for that category of dwelling increased by 1 per cent. where that is lower than or equal to the rent at the 30th percentile determined in accordance with sub-paragraphs (4) to (8).

(4) The rent officer must compile a list of rents in ascending order of the rents which, in the rent officer's opinion, are payable—
- (a) for a dwelling let under an assured tenancy for each category of dwelling specified in paragraph 1; and
- (b) in the 12 month period ending on the 30th day of the September preceding the date of the determination.

(5) In compiling the list of rents, the rent officer must—
- (a) include within it the rent of an assured tenancy in relation to each category of dwelling if—
  - (i) the dwelling let under the assured tenancy is in the broad rental market area for which the local housing allowance for that category of dwelling is being determined;
  - (ii) the dwelling is in a reasonable state of repair; and
  - (iii) the assured tenancy permits the tenant to use exclusively or share the use of, as the case may be, the same number and type of rooms as the category of dwelling in relation to which the list is being compiled;
- (b) include within it any rents which are of the same amount;
- (c) where rent is payable other than weekly, use the figure which would be payable if the rent were to be payable weekly by—
  - (i) multiplying the rent by an appropriate figure to obtain the rent for a year;
  - (ii) dividing the total in (i) by 365; and
  - (iii) multiplying the total in (ii) by 7;
- (d) assume that no one who would have been entitled to housing benefit had sought or is seeking the tenancy; and
- (e) exclude the amount of any rent which, in the rent officer's opinion, is fairly attributable to the provision of services performed for, or facilities (including the use of furniture) provided for, or rights made available to, the tenant which are ineligible to be met by housing benefit.

(6) Sub-paragraph (7) applies where the rent officer is not satisfied that the list of rents in respect of any category of dwelling would contain sufficient rents, payable in the 12 month period ending on the 30th day of the September preceding the date of the determination for dwellings in the broad rental market area, to enable a local housing allowance to be determined which is representative of the rents that a landlord might reasonably be expected to obtain in that area.

(7) In a case where this sub-paragraph applies the rent officer may add to the list rents for dwellings in the same category in other areas in which a comparable market exists.

(8) The rent officer must use the list of rents to determine the rent at the 30th percentile in the list ("R") by—
- (a) where the number of rents on the list is a multiple of 10, applying the formula—

$$R = \frac{\text{the amount of the rent at P} + \text{the amount of the rent at P1}}{2}$$

Where—
- (i) P is the position on the list found by multiplying the number of rents on the list by 3 and dividing by 10; and
- (ii) P1 is the following position on the list;
- (b) where the number of rents on the list is not a multiple of 10, applying the formula—

$$R = \text{the amount of the rent at P2}$$

Where—
P2 is the position on the list found by multiplying the number of rents on the list by 3 and dividing by 10 and rounding the result upwards to the nearest whole number.

(9) The maximum local housing allowance for each category of dwelling specified in the paragraph of this Schedule listed in column (1) is the amount specified for that category of dwelling in column (2).

(1) Paragraph of this Schedule defining the category of dwelling	(2) Maximum local housing allowance for that category of dwelling
paragraph 1(1)(a) (one bedroom, shared accommodation)	£258.06
paragraph 1(1)(b) (one bedroom, exclusive use)	£258.06
paragraph 1(1)(c) (two bedrooms)	£299.34

Rent Officers (HB and UC Functions) (Local Housing Allowance Amendments) Order 2013

paragraph 1(1)(d) (three bedrooms) £350.95
paragraph 1(1)(e) (four bedrooms) £412.89

(10) Where the local housing allowance would otherwise not be a whole number of pence, it must be rounded to the nearest whole penny by disregarding any amount less than half a penny and treating any amount of half a penny or more as a whole penny.".

(3) After paragraph 5 insert–

"6. The table referred to in paragraph 2(2) of this Schedule is below.

(1) Broad rental market area	(2) Paragraph of this Schedule defining the category of dwelling
Aberdeen and Shire	paragraph 1(1)(a) (one bedroom, shared accommodation)
	paragraph 1(1)(c) (two bedrooms)
	paragraph 1(1)(d) (three bedrooms)
	paragraph 1(1)(e) (four bedrooms)
Argyll and Bute	paragraph 1(1)(b) (one bedroom, exclusive use)
Fife	paragraph 1(1)(a) (one bedroom, shared accommodation)
Forth Valley	paragraph 1(1)(e) (four bedrooms)
Greater Glasgow	paragraph 1(1)(a) (one bedroom, shared accommodation)
Scottish Borders	paragraph 1(1)(a) (one bedroom, shared accommodation)".

The Age-Related Payments Regulations 2013
(SI 2013 No.2980)

Made   27th November 2013
Coming into force in accordance with regulation 1(1)

The Treasury make the following Regulations in exercise of the powers conferred by section 7(1), (1A), (2) and (3) of the Age-Related Payments Act 2004 now vested in them by the Transfer of Functions (Age-Related Payments) Order 2013.

In accordance with section 7(4)(b) of the Age-Related Payments Act 2004, a draft of these Regulations has been laid before Parliament and approved by a resolution of each House of Parliament.

Citation, commencement and interpretation

1.–(1) These Regulations may be cited as the Age-Related Payments Regulations 2013 and come into force on the day after the day on which they are made.
(2) *[Omitted]*

Entitlement: payments to qualifying Equitable Life annuitants

2.–(1) A qualifying Equitable Life annuitant ("A") is entitled to a payment of £5000 under this regulation.
(2)–(8) *[Omitted]*

Entitlement: payments to qualifying Equitable Life annuitants in receipt of pension credit or similar benefit

3.–(1) A qualifying Equitable Life annuitant ("A") is entitled to a payment of £5000 under this regulation in addition to a payment under regulation 2(1) if A was in receipt of state pension credit on 1st November 2013.
(2)–(8) *[Omitted]*

Payment to be disregarded for tax and social security

5. Section 6 of the Age-Related Payments Act 2004 applies to a payment made under these Regulations as it applies to a payment made under that Act.

The Council Tax Reduction Schemes (Prescribed Requirements) (England) (Amendment) Regulations 2013
(SI 2013 No.3181)

Made   *16th December 2013*
Laid before Parliament   *20th December 2013*
Coming into force   *13th January 2014*

The Secretary of State makes the following Regulations in exercise of the powers conferred by section 113(1) and (2) of, and paragraph 2 of Schedule 1A to, the Local Government Finance Act 1992:

Citation, commencement and application
1.–(1) These Regulations may be cited as the Council Tax Reduction Schemes (Prescribed Requirements) (England) (Amendment) Regulations 2013 and come into force on 13th January 2014.
(2) These Regulations apply in relation to council tax reduction schemes made by billing authorities for financial years beginning on or after 1st April 2014.

Amendments to the Council Tax Reduction Schemes (Prescribed Requirements) (England) Regulations 2012
2.–(1) The Council Tax Reduction Schemes (Prescribed Requirements) (England) Regulations 2012 are amended as follows.
(2) In regulation 2(1) (interpretation) after "Scottish Parliament" in the definition of "enactment" insert "or the National Assembly for Wales".
(3) In regulation 3(a)(ii) (meaning of "pensioner") for "he is not, or," substitute "he is not and,".
(4) In regulation 8 (households)–
(a) in paragraph (2)(a) after "boarded out" insert "or placed";
(b) in paragraph (5)–
   (i) omit "and" after sub-paragraph (n);
   (ii) after sub-paragraph (n) insert–

"(na) the Children's Hearings (Scotland) Act 2011; and".

(5) In regulation 12 (persons treated as not being in Great Britain)–
(a) before "or" at the end of sub-paragraph (a) in paragraph (4) insert–

"(aa) regulation 14 of the EEA Regulations, but only in a case where the right exists under that regulation because the person is–
   (i) a jobseeker for the purpose of the definition of "qualified person" in regulation 6(1) of those Regulations, or
   (ii) a family member (within the meaning of regulation 7 of those Regulations) of such a jobseeker;
(ab) Article 45 of the Treaty on the functioning of the European Union (in a case where the person is seeking work in the United Kingdom, the Channel Islands, the Isle of Man or the Republic of Ireland);";

(b) in paragraph (5)–
   (i) for sub-paragraph (e) substitute–

"(e) a person who has been granted, or who is deemed to have been granted, leave outside the rules made under section 3(2) of the Immigration Act 1971 where that leave is–
   (i) discretionary leave to enter or remain in the United Kingdom,
   (ii) leave to remain under the Destitution Domestic Violence concession which came into effect on 1st April 2012, or

(iii) leave deemed to have been granted by virtue of regulation 3 of the Displaced Persons (Temporary Protection) Regulations 2005;";

(ii) omit "or" after sub-paragraph (f); and
(iii) after sub-paragraph (g) insert–

"(h) in receipt of income support, an income-based jobseeker's allowance or on an income-related employment and support allowance; or
(i) a person who is treated as a worker for the purpose of the definition of "qualified person" in regulation 6(1) of the EEA Regulations pursuant to regulation 5 of the Accession of Croatia (Immigration and Worker Authorisation) Regulations 2013 (right of residence of a Croatian who is an "accession State national subject to worker authorisation")''.

(6) In regulation 13 (persons subject to immigration control)–
(a) at the beginning of paragraph (1) insert "Subject to paragraph (1A),";
(b) after paragraph (1) insert–

"(1A) A person who is a national of a state which has ratified the European Convention on Social and Medical Assistance(f) (done in Paris on 11th December 1953) or a state which has ratified the Council of Europe Social Charter (signed in Turin on 18th October 1961) and who is lawfully present in the United Kingdom is not a person subject to immigration control for the purpose of paragraph (1).".

(7) In Schedule 1 (pensioners: matters to be included in schemes)–
(a) in the heading to paragraph 2 (class A: pensioners whose income is less than the applicable amount) for "is less than" substitute "is no greater than";
(b) in paragraph 6(2) (applicable amounts) for the definition of "additional spouse" substitute–

"additional spouse" means a spouse of either party to the marriage who is additional to the other party to the marriage;";

(a) in paragraph 8 (non-dependant deductions)–
(i)–(v) *[Omitted]*
(vi) at the end of sub-paragraph (7) add–

"(e) he is not residing with the applicant because he is a member of the regular forces or the reserve forces (within the meaning of section 374 of the Armed Forces Act 2006) who is absent, while on operations, from the dwelling usually occupied as their home.";

(b) in paragraph 25(14) (treatment of child care charges) for "sub-paragraph (16)" substitute "sub-paragraph (15)".
(8) *[Omitted]*
(9) *[Omitted]*
(10) In paragraph 3(2) of Schedule 4 (sums disregarded from applicant's earnings) for paragraph (b) substitute–

"(b) a part-time fire-fighter employed by the Scottish Fire and Rescue Service established under section 1A of the Fire (Scotland) Act 2005;".

(11) *[Omitted]*
(12) In Schedule 6 (capital disregards)–
(a) in paragraph 21–
(i) after sub-paragraph (1)(e) insert–

"(f) by way of occasional assistance including arrears and payments in lieu of occasional assistance (and in this paragraph "occasional assistance" has the same meaning as in paragraph 16 of Schedule 1)";

(ii) at the end of sub-paragraph (2)(n) omit "or";
(iii) at the end of sub-paragraph (2)(o) insert "or";

(iv) after sub-paragraph (2)(o) insert–

"(p) social fund payments under Part 8 of the SSCBA.";

(b) in paragraph 22 after sub-paragraph (2)(e) insert–

"(f) paragraph 18 of Schedule 10 to the Universal Credit Regulations 2013;";

(c) after paragraph 29 insert–

"**29A.** A payment made under the Age-Related Payments Regulations 2013(c).".

(13) In paragraph 9(1) of Schedule 8 (duty to notify change of circumstances) for "Subject to sub-paragraphs (3), (6) and (7)" substitute "Subject to sub-paragraphs (3) and (9)".

The Marriage (Same Sex Couples) Act 2013 (Consequential Provisions) Order 2014

(SI 2014 No.107)

Made   *20th January 2014*
Laid before Parliament   *23rd January 2014*
Coming into force   *13th March 2014*

This Order is made in exercise of the powers conferred by sections 17(2) and (3) and 18(10) of the Marriage (Same Sex Couples) Act 2013 and by section 259(1) and (4) of the Civil Partnership Act 2004.

The Secretary of State, in exercise of those powers, makes the following Order:

Citation, commencement, interpretation and extent

1.–(1) This Order may be cited as the Marriage (Same Sex Couples) Act 2013 (Consequential Provisions) Order 2014.
(2) This Order comes into force on 13th March 2014.
(3) In this Order "the Act" means the Marriage (Same Sex Couples) Act 2013.
(4) Subject to paragraph (5), this Order extends to England and Wales only.
(5) Paragraphs 18(2)(b) and (3)(b) and 19 of Schedule 1 extend also to Scotland.

Amendments to subordinate legislation

2. Schedule 1 (which amends subordinate legislation in consequence of the Act and the Civil Partnership Act 2004) has effect.

SCHEDULE 1 ARTICLE 2

CONSEQUENTIAL AMENDMENTS TO SUBORDINATE LEGISLATION

Housing Benefit and Council Tax Benefit (Decisions and Appeals) Regulations 2001
30. In regulation 1(2) of the Housing Benefit and Council Tax Benefit (Decisions and Appeals) Regulations 2001 (interpretation), for the definition of "couple" substitute–

"couple" means–
(a) two people who are married to, or civil partners of, each other and are members of the same household; or
(b) two people who are not married to, or civil partners of, each other but are living together as a married couple;".

Housing Benefit Regulations 2006
40. In regulation 2(1) of the Housing Benefit Regulations 2006 (interpretation), for the definition of "couple" substitute–

"couple" means–
(a) two people who are married to, or civil partners of, each other and are members of the same household; or
(b) two people who are not married to, or civil partners of, each other but are living together as a married couple;".

Housing Benefit (Persons who have attained the qualifying age for state pension credit) Regulations 2006
41. In regulation 2(1) of the Housing Benefit (Persons who have attained the qualifying age for state pension credit) Regulations 2006(b) (interpretation), for the definition of "couple" substitute–

"couple" means–
(a) two people who are married to, or civil partners of, each other and are members of the same household; or
(b) two people who are not married to, or civil partners of, each other but are living together as a married couple;".

Council Tax Reduction Schemes (Prescribed Requirements) (England) Regulations 2012

54. In the Council Tax Reduction Schemes (Prescribed Requirements) (England) Regulations 2012, for regulation 4 (meaning of "couple") substitute–

"**Meaning of "couple"**

4. In these Regulations, "couple" means–
(a) two people who are married to, or civil partners of, each other and are members of the same household; or
(b) two people who are not married to, or civil partners of, each other but are living together as a married couple.".

The Housing Benefit (Transitional Provisions) (Amendment) Regulations 2014
(SI 2014 No.212)

Made   *4th February 2014*
Laid before Parliament   *5th February 2014*
Coming into force   *3rd March 2014*

The Secretary of State for Work and Pensions makes the following Regulations in exercise of the powers conferred by sections 123(1)(d), 130A(2) to (5), 137(1) and 175(1), (3) and (4) of the Social Security Contributions and Benefits Act 1992.

In accordance with section 173(1)(b) of the Social Security Administration Act 1992, the Secretary of State has obtained the agreement of the Social Security Advisory Committee that the proposals in respect of these Regulations should not be referred to it.

In accordance with section 176(1) of the Social Security Administration Act 1992, the Secretary of State has consulted with organisations appearing to him to be representative of the authorities concerned.

Citation and commencement

1. These Regulations may be cited as the Housing Benefit (Transitional Provisions) (Amendment) Regulations 2014 and come into force on 3rd March 2014.

Amendment of the Housing Benefit and Council Tax Benefit (Consequential Provisions) Regulations 2006

2.–(1) Paragraph 4 of Schedule 3 (transitional and savings provisions) to the Housing Benefit and Council Tax Benefit (Consequential Provisions) Regulations 2006 is amended as follows.

(2) In sub-paragraph (2)–
(a) at the end of paragraph (a) omit "or";
(b) after paragraph (a) insert–

"(aa) a determination of eligible rent in a case where a person's landlord is a registered housing association within the meaning of regulation 2 of the Housing Benefit Regulations or any case where housing benefit is payable in the form of a rent rebate unless–
(i) the claimant or the claimant's partner has attained the qualifying age for state pension credit, or both have attained that age;
(ii) a relevant authority has, on or before 31st March 2013, reduced that person's eligible rent in accordance with regulation 13(3) of the Housing Benefit Regulations as set out in paragraph 5 of this Schedule; or
(iii) a relevant authority has, on or before 31st March 2013, made a determination that the person's dwelling is larger than is reasonably required or that the person's rent is unreasonably high in accordance with regulation 13(3) of the Housing Benefit Regulations as set out in paragraph 5 of this Schedule, but has not, in accordance with paragraph (4), (5) or (7) of that regulation, reduced that person's eligible rent; or".

(3) In paragraph (a) of the definition of "eligible rent" in sub-paragraph (10), after "regulations 12B (eligible rent)," insert "12BA (eligible rent and maximum rent (social sector)),".

Amendment of the Housing Benefit Regulations 2006

3.–(1) Paragraph (1) of regulation A13 (when a maximum rent (social sector) is to be determined) of the Housing Benefit Regulations 2006(a) is amended as follows–
(a) at the end of paragraph (1)(a) omit the "or"; and
(b) after paragraph (1)(b) insert–

"; or
an eligible rent in a case where paragraph 4 of Schedule 3 (transitional and savings provisions) to the Consequential Provisions Regulations applies.".

The Housing Benefit (Miscellaneous Amendments) Regulations 2014
(SI 2014 No.213)

Made   *30th January 2014*
Laid before Parliament   *6th February 2014*
Coming into force in accordance with regulation 1

The Secretary of State for Work and Pensions makes the following Regulations in exercise of the powers conferred by sections 123(1)(d), 130A(2), (3) and (4), 135(1) and (6), 136(3) and (4), 137(1) and 175(1) and (3) of the Social Security Contributions and Benefits Act 1992, sections 5(1)(a) and 189(1), (4) and (6) of the Social Security Administration Act 1992, section 79(4) of the Social Security Act 1998 and paragraphs 4(4) and (6), 20(1) and 23(1) of Schedule 7 to the Child Support, Pensions and Social Security Act 2000.

In accordance with section 173(1)(b) of the Social Security Administration Act 1992, the Secretary of State has obtained the agreement of the Social Security Advisory Committee that the proposals in respect of these Regulations should not be referred to it.

In accordance with section 176(1) of the Social Security Administration Act 1992, the Secretary of State has consulted with organisations appearing to him to be representative of the authorities concerned.

Citation and commencement

1.–(1) These Regulations may be cited as the Housing Benefit (Miscellaneous Amendments) Regulations 2014.
(2) This regulation and regulation 2 come into force on 31st March 2014.
(3) Regulations 3 and 4 come into force–
(a) in relation to any case where rent is payable at intervals of a week or any multiple of a week, on 7th April 2014; or
(b) in relation to any other case, on 1st April 2014.

Amendment of the Housing Benefit and Council Tax Benefit (Decisions and Appeals) Regulations 2001

2.–(1) The Housing Benefit and Council Tax Benefit (Decisions and Appeals) Regulations 2001 are amended as follows.
(2) In regulation 7(2) (decisions superseding earlier decisions)–
(a) in sub-paragraph (i) for "or (q)" substitute ", (q) or (s)";
(b) after sub-paragraph (r) add–

"(s) which is affected by the award of personal independence payment under Part 4 of the Welfare Reform Act 2012 where–
(i) the claimant, the claimant's partner or a member of the claimant's family ("P") was entitled to disability living allowance under section 71 of the Social Security Contributions and Benefits Act 1992; and
(ii) subsequent to the first day of the period to which the claimant's entitlement to housing benefit relates, P becomes entitled to personal independence payment as a transfer claimant (within the meaning of regulation 2(1) of the Personal Independence Payment (Transitional Provisions) Regulations 2013.".

(3) In regulation 8 (date from which a decision superseding an earlier decision takes effect) after paragraph (14F) add–

"(14G) A superseding decision made in consequence of regulation 7(2)(s) shall take effect–
(a) on 1st April in a case where–
(i) the claimant's weekly amount of eligible rent falls to be calculated in accordance with regulation 80(2)(b) or (c) of the Housing Benefit

(SI 2014 No.213, reg 3)

    Regulations or, as the case may be, regulation 61(2)(b) or (c) of the Housing Benefit (State Pension Credit) Regulations; and
  (ii) the decision to award personal independence payment takes effect in the same benefit week as the 1st April;
(b) on the first Monday in April in a case where–
  (i) the claimant's weekly amount of eligible rent falls to be calculated in accordance with regulation 80(2)(a) of the Housing Benefit Regulations or, as the case may be, regulation 61(2)(a) of the Housing Benefit (State Pension Credit) Regulations; and
  (ii) the decision to award personal independence payment takes effect in the same benefit week as the first Monday in April;
(c) in ay other case, on the day after the last day of entitlement to disability living allowance.".

Amendment of the Housing Benefit Regulations 2006

3.–(1) The Housing Benefit Regulations 2006 are amended as follows.
(2) In regulation 2(1) (interpretation)(a) in the definition of "young individual"–
(a) at the end of paragraph (h) omit "or";
(b) renumber as paragraph (j) the paragraph (i) added by regulation 2(2)(b)(ii) of the Housing Benefit and Universal Credit (Size Criteria) (Miscellaneous Amendments) Regulations 2013;
(c) after the paragraph (i) added by paragraph 23(3) of Schedule 1 to the Children's Hearings (Scotland) Act 2011 (Consequential and Transitional Provisions and Savings) Order 2013 add "or".
(3) In regulation 28 (treatment of child care charges)–
(a) in paragraph 11(e) for "or allowance to which head (ii), (iv), (v) or (vi)" substitute ", allowance or payment to which head (ii), (iv), (v), (vi) or (viii)";
(b) in paragraph (13)(d) for "would be payable but for" substitute "has ceased to be payable solely by virtue of".
(4) In the following provisions for "social security contributions" substitute "national insurance contributions"–
(a) regulation 34(c) (disregard of changes in tax, contributions etc);
(b) in regulation 38 (calculation of net profit of self-employed earners)–
  (i) paragraph (1)(b)(i);
  (ii) paragraph (3)(b)(ii);
  (iii) paragraph (9)(a)(ii);
(c) regulation 39(2) (deduction of tax and contributions of self-employed earners).
(5) In regulation 87(1) (amendment and withdrawal of claim) for "determination" substitute "decision".
(6) In Schedule 3 (applicable amounts)–
(a) in paragraph 13 (Additional Condition for the Disability Premium) for sub-paragraph (1)(a)(iiia) substitute–

"(iiia) was in receipt of personal independence payment that is no longer payable by virtue of regulations made under section 86(1) (hospital in-patients) of the 2012 Act.";

(b) in paragraph 14 (Severe Disability Premium) in sub-paragraph (5)(c) after "but for" insert "payment ceasing by virtue of";
(c) in paragraph 15 (Enhanced disability premium) in sub-paragraph (1)(c) for ", or would, but for regulations made under section 86(1) (hospital in-patients) of the 2012 Act be payable" substitute "payable, or has ceased to be payable by virtue of regulations made under section 86(1) (hospital in-patients) of the 2012 Act,";
(d) in paragraph 16 (Disabled child premium) in paragraph (d) after "but for" insert "payment ceasing by virtue of".

Amendment of the Housing Benefit (Persons who have attained the qualifying age for state pension credit) Regulations 2006

4.–(1) The Housing Benefit (Persons who have attained the qualifying age for state pension credit) Regulations 2006 are amended as follows.

(2) In regulation 31(treatment of child care charges)–
- (a) in paragraph 11(e) for "or allowance to which head (ii), (iv), (v) or (vi)" substitute ", allowance or payment to which head (ii), (iv), (v), (vi) or (viii)";
- (b) in paragraph (13)(d) for "would be payable but for" substitute "has ceased to be payable solely by virtue of".

(3) In the following provisions for "social security contributions" substitute "national insurance contributions"–
- (a) regulation 34(c) (disregard of changes in tax, contributions etc);
- (b) in regulation 39 (calculation of net profit of self-employed earners)–
   - (i) paragraph (1)(b)(i);
   - (ii) paragraph (2)(b)(ii);
   - (iii) paragraph (8)(a)(ii);
- (c) regulation 40(2) (deduction of tax and contributions of self-employed earners).

(4) In regulation 68(1) (amendment and withdrawal of claim) for "determination" substitute "decision".

(5) In Schedule 3 (applicable amounts)–
- (a) in paragraph 6 (Severe disability premium) in sub-paragraph (7)(c) after "but for" insert "payment ceasing by virtue of";
- (b) in paragraph 7 (Enhanced disability premium) in sub-paragraph (1)(b) for ", or would, but for" substitute "payable, or has ceased to be payable by virtue of";
- (c) in paragraph 8 (Disabled child premium) in paragraph (d) after "but for" insert "payment ceasing by virtue of".

The Social Care (Self-directed Support) (Scotland) Act 2013 (Consequential Modifications and Savings) Order 2014

(SI 2014 No.513)

Made	4th March 2014
Laid	6th March 2014
Coming into force	1st April 2014

The Secretary of State makes the following Order in exercise of the powers conferred by sections 104, 112(1) and 113(2), (4) and (5) of the Scotland Act 1998.

Citation, commencement and extent

1.–(1) This Order may be cited as the Social Care (Self-directed Support) (Scotland) Act 2013 (Consequential Modifications and Savings) Order 2014.

(2) This Order comes into force on 1st April 2014.

(3) Any modification made by the Schedule has the same extent as the provision being modified.

Modifications

2. The modifications contained in the Schedule have effect.

Savings

3. Notwithstanding article 2, the modifications contained in the Schedule are of no effect in respect of a payment made under section 12B of the Social Work (Scotland) Act 1968(a) after this Order comes into force.

SCHEDULE Article 2

MODIFICATIONS

Housing Benefit Regulations 2006

10. In–
(a) paragraph 57 of Schedule 5 (sums to be disregarded in the calculation of income other than earnings); and
(b) paragraph 58 of Schedule 6 (capital to be disregarded), to the Housing Benefit Regulations 2006, for "under section 12B of the Social Work (Scotland) Act 1968" substitute "as a direct payment as defined in section 4(2) of the Social Care (Self-directed Support) (Scotland) Act 2013".

Housing Benefit (Persons who have attained the qualifying age for state pension credit) Regulations 2006

11. In paragraph 26D of Part 1 (capital to be disregarded generally) of Schedule 6 (capital to be disregarded) to the Housing Benefit (Persons who have attained the qualifying age for state pension credit) Regulations 2006–
(a) omit "by virtue of regulations made under";
(b) at the beginning of paragraphs (a) and (c) insert "by virtue of regulations made under"; and
(c) for paragraph (b) substitute–

"(b) as a direct payment as defined in section 4(2) of the Social Care (Self-directed Support) (Scotland) Act 2013; or".

Council Tax Reduction Schemes (Prescribed Requirements) (England) Regulations 2012

22. In Schedule 6 (capital disregards) to the Council Tax Reduction Schemes (Prescribed Requirements) (England) Regulations 2012–
(a) in paragraph 29, omit paragraph (b); and
(b) after paragraph 29 insert–

"**29ZA.** Any payment made as a direct payment as defined in section 4(2) of the Social Care (Self-directed Support) (Scotland) Act 2013.".

Council Tax Reduction Schemes and Prescribed Requirements (Wales) Regulations 2013

25.—(1) The Council Tax Reduction Schemes and Prescribed Requirements (Wales) Regulations 2013 are amended as follows.

(2) In paragraph 28 of Schedule 5 (capital disregards: pensioners), omit paragraph (b).

(3) After paragraph 28 of Schedule 5 insert—

(a) in the English text—

"**28A.** Any payment made as a direct payment as defined in section 4(2) of the Social Care (Self-directed Support) (Scotland) Act 2013."; and

(b) in the Welsh text—

"**28A.** Unrhyw daliad a wneir ar ffurf taliad uniongyrchol fel y'i diffinnir yn adran 4(2) o Ddeddf Gofal Cymdeithasol (Cymorth Hunangyfeiriedig) (Yr Alban) 2013.".

(4) In paragraph 59 of Schedule 9 (sums disregarded in the calculation of income other than earnings: persons who are not pensioners) and paragraph 60 of Schedule 10 (capital disregards: persons who are not pensioners)—

(a) in the English text, for "under section 12B of the Social Work (Scotland) Act 1968" substitute "as a direct payment as defined in section 4(2) of the Social Care (Self-directed Support) (Scotland) Act 2013"; and

(b) in the Welsh text, for "o dan adran 12B o Ddeddf Gwaith Cymdeithasol (Yr Alban) 1968" substitute "ar ffurf taliad uniongyrchol fel y'i diffinnir yn adran 4(2) o Ddeddf Gofal Cymdeithasol (Cymorth Hunangyfeiriedig) (Yr Alban) 2013".

Council Tax Reduction Schemes (Default Scheme) (Wales) Regulations 2013

26.—(1) The scheme set out in the Schedule to the Council Tax Reduction Schemes (Default Scheme) (Wales) Regulations 2013 is amended as follows.

(2) In paragraph 59 of Schedule 7 (sums disregarded in the calculation of income other than earnings: persons who are not pensioners)—

(a) in the English text, for "under section 12B of the Social Work (Scotland) Act 1968" substitute "as a direct payment as defined in section 4(2) of the Social Care (Self-directed Support) (Scotland) Act 2013"; and

(b) in the Welsh text, for "o dan adran 12B o Ddeddf Gwaith Cymdeithasol (Yr Alban) 1968" substitute "ar ffurf taliad uniongyrchol fel y'i diffinnir yn adran 4(2) o Ddeddf Gofal Cymdeithasol (Cymorth Hunangyfeiriedig) (Yr Alban) 2013".

(3) In paragraph 28 of Part 1 of Schedule 8 (capital to be disregarded), omit paragraph (b).

(4) After paragraph 28 of Schedule 8 insert—

(a) in the English text—

"**28A.** Any payment made as a direct payment as defined in section 4(2) of the Social Care (Self-directed Support) (Scotland) Act 2013."; and

(b) in the Welsh text—

"**28A.** Unrhyw daliad a wneir ar ffurf taliad uniongyrchol fel y'i diffinnir yn adran 4(2) o Ddeddf Gofal Cymdeithasol (Cymorth Hunangyfeiriedig) (Yr Alban) 2013.".

(5) In paragraph 60 of Schedule 9 (capital disregards: persons who are not pensioners)—

(a) in the English text, for "section 12B of the Social Work (Scotland) Act 1968" substitute "as a direct payment as defined in section 4(2) of the Social Care (Self-directed Support) (Scotland) Act 2013"; and

(b) in the Welsh text, for "o dan adran 12B o Ddeddf Gwaith Cymdeithasol (Yr Alban) 1968" substitute "ar ffurf taliad uniongyrchol fel y'i diffinnir yn adran 4(2) o Ddeddf Gofal Cymdeithasol (Cymorth Hunangyfeiriedig) (Yr Alban) 2013".

The Housing Benefit (Habitual Residence) Amendment Regulations 2014

(SI 2014 No.539)

Made   *5th March 2014*
Laid before Parliament   *11th March 2014*
Coming into force   *1st April 2014*

The Secretary of State for Work and Pensions makes the following Regulations in exercise of the powers conferred by sections 123(1)(d), 137(1) and (2)(i) and 175(1), (3) and (4) of the Social Security Contributions and Benefits Act 1992.

The Secretary of State has not referred proposals in respect of these Regulations to the Social Security Advisory Committee, as it appears to him that by reason of the urgency of the matter it is inexpedient to do so.

The Secretary of State has not undertaken consultation with organisations appearing to him to be representative of the authorities concerned, as it appears to him that by reason of the urgency of the matter it is inexpedient to do so.

Citation and commencement
1. These Regulations may be cited as the Housing Benefit (Habitual Residence) Amendment Regulations 2014 and come into force on 1st April 2014.

Amendment of the Housing Benefit Regulations 2006
2.–(1) In regulation 10(3B) of the Housing Benefit Regulations 2006–
(a) omit the "or" following sub-paragraph (i);
(b) in sub-paragraph (k) omit '', an income-based jobseeker's allowance";
(c) after sub-paragraph (k) add–

'';or
(l) in receipt of an income-based jobseeker's allowance and has a right to reside other than a right to reside falling within paragraph (3A).".

Saving
3.–(1) The amendment in regulation 2 does not apply to a person who, on 31st March 2014, is entitled to–
(a) housing benefit; and
(b) an income-based jobseeker's allowance, until the first of the events in paragraph (2) occurs.
(2) The events are–
(a) the person ceases to be entitled to that income-based jobseeker's allowance; or
(b) the person makes a new claim for housing benefit.

The Marriage (Same Sex Couples) Act 2013 (Consequential and Contrary Provisions and Scotland) Order 2014

(SI 2014 No.560)

Made   6th March 2014
Coming into force in accordance with article 1(2) and (3)

A draft of this Order was laid before and approved by a resolution of each House of Parliament in accordance with section 18(2) of the Marriage (Same Sex Couples) Act 2013, section 259(8) of the Civil Partnership Act 2004 and section 62(3) of the Human Fertilisation and Embryology Act 2008.

In accordance with section 18(11)(a) of the Marriage (Same Sex Couples) Act 2013, the Secretary of State has obtained the consent of the Scottish Ministers to the making of article 5 of, and paragraph 31 of Schedule 1 to, this Order.

This Order is made in exercise of the powers conferred by sections 17(2), (3) and 18(10) of, and paragraph 1(1) of Schedule 2 and paragraph 27(3)(a) and (b) of Schedule 4 to, the Marriage (Same Sex Couples) Act 2013, and in exercise of the powers conferred by section 259(1) and (3) of the Civil Partnership Act 2004 and by section 64(1) and (2) of the Human Fertilisation and Embryology Act 2008.

The Secretary of State, in exercise of those powers, makes the following Order:

Citation, commencement and interpretation

1.–(1) This Order may be cited as the Marriage (Same Sex Couples) Act 2013 (Consequential and Contrary Provisions and Scotland) Order 2014.
 (2) Subject to paragraph (3), this Order comes into force on 13th March 2014.
 (3) The amendment made to the Family Law (Scotland) Act 2006(d) at paragraph 31 of Schedule 1 comes into force on 3rd June 2014.
 (4) In this Order–
"the Act" means the Marriage (Same Sex Couples) Act 2013; and
"the 2004 Act" means the Civil Partnership Act 2004.

Consequential amendments to Acts of Parliament

2. Schedule 1 to this Order (which amends primary legislation in consequence of the Act, the 2004 Act and the Human Fertilisation and Embryology Act 2008) has effect.

Contrary provision to section 11(1) and (2) of, and paragraphs 1 to 3 of Schedule 3 to, the Act

3. Schedule 2 to this Order (which makes provision to which section 11(1) and (2) of, and paragraphs 1 to 3 of Schedule 3 to, the Act are subject and which disapplies that section and those paragraphs in specified cases) has effect.

Consequential amendments to enactments etc. as a result of contrary provision made by Schedule 2

4. Schedule 3 to this Order (which makes amendments to enactments etc. in consequence of the provision made by Schedule 2 to this Order) has effect.

Scotland

5. Under the law of Scotland, a marriage of a same sex couple under the law of England and Wales is to be treated as a civil partnership formed under the law of England and Wales, and accordingly, the spouses are to be treated as civil partners.

Extent

6.–(1) Subject to paragraphs (2) to (4), this Order extends to England and Wales only.
 (2) The amendment to the Family Law (Scotland) Act 2006 at paragraph 31 of Schedule 1, and article 2 so far as it relates to that paragraph, extend to Scotland only.

(3) The following provisions extend also to Scotland–
(a) article 1,
(b) the amendment to the 2004 Act at paragraph 29(1) and (2) of Schedule 1, and article 2 so far as it relates to that paragraph, article 5, and
(c) this article.
(4) The following provisions extend also to Northern Ireland–
(a) article 1,
(b) the amendment to the 2004 Act at paragraph 29(1) and (2) of Schedule 1, and article 2 so far as it relates to that paragraph, and
this article.

SCHEDULE 1 ARTICLE 2
CONSEQUENTIAL AMENDMENTS TO PRIMARY LEGISLATION

Social Security Contributions and Benefits Act 1992
22.–(1) The Social Security Contributions and Benefits Act 1992 is amended as follows.
(2)–(7) *[Omitted]*
(8) In section 137 (interpretation of Part 7 and supplementary provisions)–
(a) in subsection (1), for the definition of "couple" substitute–

''"couple" means–
(a) two people who are married to, or civil partners of, each other and are members of the same household; or
(b) two people who are not married to, or civil partners of, each other but are living together as a married couple otherwise than in prescribed circumstances;", and

(b) omit subsection (1A).
(9) *[Omitted]*

The Social Security (Miscellaneous Amendments) Regulations 2014
(SI 2014 No.591)

Made	11th March 2014
Laid before Parliament	18th March 2014
Coming into force	28th April 2014

The Secretary of State for Work and Pensions makes the following Regulations in exercise of the powers conferred by sections 44C(3)(e), 123(1)(a) and (d), 136(3), (4) and (5), 136A, 137(1) and 175(1), (3) and (4) of the Social Security Contributions and Benefits Act 1992, sections 5(1)(a), 115A(2)(b), 189(1), (4) and (6) and 191 of the Social Security Administration Act 1992 ("the Administration Act"), sections 12(4), 35(1), 36(1), (2) and (4)(a) of the Jobseekers Act 1995, sections 15(3) and (6), 17(1) and 19(1) of the State Pension Credit Act 2002 and sections 17(1), 24(1) and 25(2), (3) and (5)(a) of the Welfare Reform Act 2007.

In accordance with section 173(1)(b) of the Administration Act, the Secretary of State has obtained the agreement of the Social Security Advisory Committee that proposals in respect of these Regulations need not be referred to it.

In respect of provisions relating to housing benefit, in accordance with section 176(1) of the Administration Act, the Secretary of State has consulted with organisations appearing to him to be representative of the authorities concerned.

Citation and commencement

1. These Regulations may be cited as the Social Security (Miscellaneous Amendments) Regulations 2014 and come into force on 28th April 2014.

Amendment of the Social Security (Penalty Notice) Regulations 1997

5.–(1) Regulation 2 (notice) of the Social Security (Penalty Notice) Regulations 1997 is amended as follows.
(2) In paragraph (1)–
(a) after "1992" insert "(''the 1992 Act") in a case to which section 115A(1) of that Act applies";
(b) in paragraph (a)–
　(i) omit "only";
　(ii) after "71,", insert "71ZB,";
(c) in paragraph (b), omit "only";
(d) in paragraph (c), for "30 per cent of the amount of the overpayment," substitute "50 per cent of the amount of the overpayment (subject to the maximum and minimum amounts prescribed in section 115A(3) of the 1992 Act)";
(e) in paragraph (d), for "28" substitute "14".
(3) After paragraph (1) insert–

"(1A) Where the Secretary of State or authority gives to a person written notice under section 115A(2) of the 1992 Act in a case to which section 115(1A) of that Act applies, the notice shall contain the information that–
(a) the penalty applies where it appears to the Secretary of State or authority that there are grounds for instituting proceedings against the person for an offence relating to an act or omission on the part of the person in relation to any benefit;
(b) if an overpayment attributable to the act or omission had been made, the overpayment would have been recoverable under section 71, 71ZB, 71A, 75 or 76 of the 1992 Act;
(c) the penalty is £350;
(d) a person who agrees to pay the penalty may withdraw the agreement within 14 days (including the date of the agreement) by notifying the Secretary of State or authority in the manner specified by the Secretary of State or authority; if the person withdraws the agreement, so much of the penalty as has already been

(e) if it is decided on review or appeal (or in accordance with regulations) that any overpayment attributable to the act or omission would not have been recoverable or due, so much of the penalty as has already been recovered shall be repaid;
(f) the payment of a penalty does not give the person immunity from prosecution in relation to any overpayment or any other offence not relating to an overpayment.".

(4) In paragraph (2), after "The notice" insert "in either case".
(5) The amendments made by paragraphs (2) to (4) apply only where the offence in respect of
which the notice is given is committed wholly on or after 8th May 2012.

Amendment of the Housing Benefit Regulations 2006

8.–(1) The Housing Benefit Regulations 2006 are amended as follows.
(2) In regulation 2 (interpretation)–
(a) in paragraph (1) omit the definition of "service user group";
(b) after paragraph (4) insert–

"(5) References in these Regulations to a claimant participating as a service user are to–
(a) a person who is being consulted by or on behalf of–
(i) a body which has a statutory duty to provide services in the field of health, social care or social housing; or
(ii) a body which conducts research or undertakes monitoring for the purpose of planning or improving such services,
in their capacity as a user, potential user, carer of a user or person otherwise affected by the provision of those services; or
(b) the carer of a person consulted under sub-paragraph (a).".

(3) In regulation 35(2)(d) (earnings of an employed earner), for "claimant's participation in a service user group" substitute "claimant participating as a service user".
(4) In regulation 42(12A) (notional income), for "claimant's participation in a service user group" substitute "claimant participating as a service user".
(5) In paragraph 2A of Schedule 5 (sums to be disregarded in the calculation of income other than earnings), for "claimant's participation in a service user group" substitute "claimant participating as a service user".

Amendment of the Housing Benefit (Persons who have attained the qualifying age for state pension credit) Regulations 2006

9.–(1) The Housing Benefit (Persons who have attained the qualifying age for state pension credit) Regulations 2006 are amended as follows.
(2) In regulation 2 (interpretation)–
(a) in paragraph (1) omit the definition of "service user group";
(b) after paragraph (5) insert–

"(6) References in these Regulations to a claimant participating as a service user are to–
(a) a person who is being consulted by or on behalf of–
(i) a body which has a statutory duty to provide services in the field of health, social care or social housing; or
(ii) a body which conducts research or undertakes monitoring for the purpose of planning or improving such services,
in their capacity as a user, potential user, carer of a user or person otherwise affected by the provision of those services; or

(b) the carer of a person consulted under sub-paragraph (a).".

(3) In regulation 35(2)(f) (earnings of employed earners), for "claimant's participation in a service user group" substitute "claimant participating as a service user".

(4) In regulation 41(8C) (notional income), for "claimant's participation in a service user group" substitute "claimant participating as a service user".

(5) In regulation 42(3) (income paid to third parties), for "claimant's participation in a service user group" substitute "claimant participating as a service user".

The Housing Benefit and Universal Credit (Supported Accommodation) (Amendment) Regulations 2014
(SI 2014 No.771)

Made *19th March 2014*
Laid before Parliament *20th March 2014*
Coming into force in accordance with regulation 1

The Secretary of State for Work and Pensions makes the following Regulations in exercise of the powers conferred by sections 11(3)(a), 42(1) and (2), 96(1), (4)(a) and (10) and 97(1) of the Welfare Reform Act 2012.

In accordance with section 173(1)(b) of the Social Security Administration Act 1992, the Secretary of State has obtained the agreement of the Social Security Advisory Committee that the proposals in respect of these Regulations should not be referred to it.

In accordance with section 176(1)(c) of the Social Security Administration Act 1992, the Secretary of State has consulted with organisations appearing to him to be representative of the authorities concerned.

Citation and commencement
1.–(1) These Regulations may be cited as the Housing Benefit and Universal Credit (Supported Accommodation) (Amendment) Regulations 2014.
(2) This regulation and regulation 3 come into force on 10th April 2014.
(3) *[Omitted]*

Amendment of the Housing Benefit Regulations 2006
3.–(1) The Housing Benefit Regulations 2006 are amended as follows.
(2) In regulation 75C(2)(a) (manner of calculating the amount of welfare benefits) for "exempt accommodation within the meaning paragraph 4(10) of Schedule 3 to the Consequential Provisions Regulations" substitute "accommodation specified in regulation 75H (specified accommodation)".
(3) After regulation 75G (interpretation) insert–

"Specified accommodation
75H.–(1) The accommodation referred to in regulation 75C(2)(a) is accommodation to which one or more of the following paragraphs applies.
(2) This paragraph applies to accommodation which is exempt accommodation within the meaning of paragraph 4(10) of Schedule 3 to the Consequential Provisions Regulations.
(3) This paragraph applies to accommodation–
(a) which is provided by a relevant body;
(b) into which the claimant has been admitted in order to meet a need for care, support or supervision; and
(c) where the claimant receives care, support or supervision.
(4) This paragraph applies to accommodation which–
(a) is provided by a relevant authority or a relevant body to the claimant because the claimant has left the home as a result of domestic violence; and
(b) consists of a building, or part of a building, which is used wholly or mainly for the non-permanent accommodation of persons who have left their homes as a result of domestic violence.
(5) This paragraph applies to accommodation–
(a) which would be a hostel within the meaning of regulation 2(1) (interpretation) but for it being owned or managed by a relevant authority; and
(b) where the claimant receives care, support or supervision.
(6) In this regulation–
"coercive behaviour" means an act of assault, humiliation or intimidation or other abuse that is used to harm, punish or frighten the victim;

"controlling behaviour" means an act designed to make a person subordinate or dependent by isolating them from sources of support, exploiting their resources and capacities for personal gain, depriving them of the means needed for independence, resistance or escape or regulating their everyday behaviour;

"domestic violence" means any incident, or pattern of incidents, of controlling behaviour, coercive behaviour, violence or abuse, including but not limited to–
  (a) psychological abuse;
  (b) physical abuse;
  (c) sexual abuse;
  (d) emotional abuse;
  (e) financial abuse,
regardless of the gender or sexuality of the victim;

"relevant body" means a–
  (a) council for a county in England for each part of whose area there is a district council;
  (b) housing association;
  (c) registered charity; or
  (d) voluntary organisation.".

The Social Security (Habitual Residence) (Amendment) Regulations 2014

(SI 2014 No.902)

Made	2nd April 2014
Laid before Parliament	8th April 2014
Coming into force	31st May 2014

The Secretary of State for Work and Pensions makes the following Regulations in exercise of the powers conferred by sections 123(1)(a) and (d), 135(1) and (2), 137(1) and 175(1) and (3) of the Social Security Contributions and Benefits Act 1992, sections 4(5) and (12), 35(1) and 36(2) of the Jobseekers Act 1995, section 115(3), (4) and (7) of the Immigration and Asylum Act 1999, sections 1(5)(a), 17(1) and 19(1) of the State Pension Credit Act 2002, sections 4(3), 24 and 25(2) and (3) of the Welfare Reform Act 2007 and sections 30, 40, 42(1), (2) and (3) of, and paragraph 7 of Schedule 1 to, the Welfare Reform Act 2012.

In accordance with section 173(1)(b) of the Social Security Administration Act 1992, the Secretary of State has obtained the agreement of the Social Security Advisory Committee that proposals in respect of these Regulations should not be referred to it.

In respect of provisions relating to housing benefit, the Secretary of State has consulted with organisations appearing to him to be representative of the authorities concerned.

Citation and commencement

1. These Regulations may be cited as the Social Security (Habitual Residence) (Amendment) Regulations 2014 and shall come into force on 31st May 2014.

Amendment of the Housing Benefit Regulations 2006

5. In Regulation 10(3B) of the Housing Benefit Regulations 2006 (persons from abroad) for sub-paragraphs (a) – (f) substitute–

"(za) a qualified person for the purposes of regulation 6 of the Immigration (European Economic Area) Regulations 2006 as a worker or a self-employed person;
(zb) a family member of a person referred to in sub-paragraph (za) within the meaning of regulation 7(1)(a), (b) or (c) of those Regulations;
(zc) a person who has a right to reside permanently in the United Kingdom by virtue of regulation 15(1)(c), (d) or (e) of those Regulations;".

Amendment of the Housing Benefit (Persons who have attained the qualifying age for state pension credit) Regulations 2006

6. In Regulation 10(4A) of the Housing Benefit (Persons who have attained the qualifying age for state pension credit) Regulations 2006 (persons from abroad) for sub-paragraphs (a) – (f) substitute–

"(za) a qualified person for the purposes of regulation 6 of the Immigration (European Economic Area) Regulations 2006 as a worker or a self-employed person;
(zb) a family member of a person referred to in sub-paragraph (za) within the meaning of regulation 7(1)(a), (b) or (c) of those Regulations;
(zc) a person who has a right to reside permanently in the United Kingdom by virtue of regulation 15(1)(c), (d) or (e) of those Regulations;".